SUCCESS STRATEGIES

For

IMMIGRANT
ENTREPRENEURS

HOW TO CREATE AND PRESERVE WEALTH
WITHOUT HEADACHES

In America

By

Ahmad Farhat

Success Strategies for Immigrant Entrepreneurs

Copyright © 2014 Ahmad Farhat

ISBN-13: 978-1505626339
ISBN-10: 1505626331

▶ | Contents

► | **Endorsements**

I met Ahmad Farhat in 2005 when I was a manager with Citigroup. Today I am CEO of a major website business. Ahmad has built a solid business by listening to the right people. Part 1 of this book reflects how he started off listening to the *wrong* people (whom he thought were giving him good business advice) and how he transformed his thoughts on how to run a business using his own ideas and philosophies. He once told me, "Not all advice is good advice."

Part 3 of this book points out that keeping clear and organized records will lead to stronger relationships with both vendor and government agencies. These strong relationships help prevent both long- and short-term issues.

In Part 2, Ahmad explains that hiring quality people, who believe in the same business philosophies, makes for a more rewarding and positive business environment. One day after he had to let go a long-time employee who was having severe attendance issues, he said, "People are assets and should be treated like assets. Poor attendance brings down company morale, and company morale is vital to our success."

I have watched his business grow during the past ten years. I have met and watched his family grow and prosper right alongside. Ahmad has also been inspirational in helping me run my current business. This book is a must read if you want the fast path to a successful business.

Jeffry Green
GM DealerFront.com

§

I have been in the banking business since 1981. I met Ahmad in 1995 at Wells Fargo Bank, where I was the branch manager. He was a young entrepreneur with big dreams and very big ambitions, looking to establish himself as well as his family. I have seen him grow into an excellent businessman and he has developed his employees to be successful in this business or any other industry they might pursue.

He is an excellent role model, and the reader will learn much by following his example. He has the determination and discipline it takes to manage a business, raise a family, be a provider, and still care and grow while managing several business locations at the same time. I consider Ahmad to be my friend as well as my client. I wish him all the success this world has to offer, and I highly recommend what he has to share with you in this book. I love the chapters on Positive Attitude and Be Open Minded, as these help on a day-to-day basis. All business-oriented people must read this book.

Silvia Zada
Vice President, Branch Manager

§

I met Ahmad Farhat more than fifteen years ago. I have seen his dedication and hard work lead him through the years to become a great entrepreneur. We have done business together with great success. I feel proud to say that I participated in the process of his first real estate purchase and many more after that.

He is a model of business management and definitely leadership, who implements dedication, consistency, and attention to details. This provides a great combination that Ahmad uses to reach success with everything he does. This book was no surprise to me. It's just additional advice from Ahmad—great advice to follow and strategies to implement. It shortens the distance to success and helps immigrant entrepreneurs reach their goals faster.

I am proud and honored to be Ahmad's friend!

Leticia Watt
Realtor/Real Estate Investor, Multi-Million-Dollar Producer
Centurion Award

§

Success Strategies for Immigrant Entrepreneurs should be mandatory for every entrepreneur who comes to the United States. As a fellow immigrant entrepreneur, the stories and experiences of Adam Farhat would have saved me a small fortune and many restless nights.

On the road to success, there are many discoveries and personal revelations, but when you could learn from someone else's mistakes, it will make your journey more enjoyable. I promise you will have to learn these success strategies sooner or later; and from my experience, later always cost more money.

I met Adam twenty years ago, and his guidance was monumental to my success. It gives me great pleasure to see him grow and evolve and to see him share his insights in his own book.

Marcos Orozco
Founder of Gentepreneur.com
Best Selling Author of Midas Mindset for Gentepreneurs

► | **Dedication**

We've all read words that have had a great impact on us—words that stick to our mind, affect our life, and make us hope that tomorrow will be better.

I dedicate these pages to Imam Ali Ibn Abi Talib, the cousin and son-in-law of the prophet Muhammad, who is known for being the gateway to knowledge.

In this book, I would like to share some words by Imam Ali Ibn Abi Talib that have had a great positive effect on my life. I will include some of these quotes in each section. These thoughts helped to open a gateway for me to wisdom and knowledge.

My favorite quotes are these two. As they have for me, I hope that they make a positive impression on the way you see life:

> Mind is the greatest wealth.

And this one:

> How strange and foolish is man.
> He loses his health in gaining wealth.
> Then to regain health he wastes his wealth.
> He ruins the present while worrying about his future,
> but weeps in the future by recalling his past.
> He lives as though death shall never come to him,
> but he dies in a way as if he were never born.

> —*Imam Ali Ibn Abi Talib*

► | Introduction

America's new immigrant entrepreneurs have created and now lead some of the world's most innovative companies. Immigrants to the United States bring a fresh perspective that can translate into new ideas for businesses. – Kauffman.org

The numbers are impressive. A 2012 study by the Fiscal Policy Institute found that among the five million small-business owners in the United States, about 900,000 were immigrants, representing about eighteen percent of the total. This percentage is higher than the immigrant share of the overall U.S. population, which is thirteen percent, and the immigrant share of the labor force, at sixteen percent. The study found that small businesses in which half or more of the owners were immigrants employed 4.7 million people in 2007, the latest year for which data were available, generating $776 billion in receipts. Between 1990 and 2010, they accounted for thirty percent of the growth in small businesses (those with fewer than one hundred employees).

Whether you're an immigrant or were born in America, succeeding as a business owner is not easy. You don't need me to tell you that most small businesses fail. According to

Introduction

Forbes Magazine, nearly eighty percent of small businesses don't make it past the first three years. If you own an online business, that number rises to ninety-five percent. It might seem that it's a bit overwhelming, but the good news is that now it's easier than ever to start your own business. The real challenge is in keeping it going!

Internet advertising and social media provide the ability to market yourself and your product to reach your customers all over the world with just a single click. It's similar to the 1849 California Gold Rush, when a lot of people were trying to get rich quickly, versus taking the time to build a strong foundation for their businesses to be productive for many years to come.

The intention of this book is to increase your probability of success as an immigrant entrepreneur. I will reveal a variety of strategies that you can implement to help you build a strong foundation and create a lasting business. My hope is that if you read this book and follow these ideas, you will avoid some of the challenges and problems that I encountered while building my successful business.

The information provided in this book is based on my personal experiences and the knowledge I have acquired throughout the years. I am proud to say that I am a successful immigrant entrepreneur who started from scratch and built my business career to realize a prosperous life for my family and me.

I am fortunate to have been involved in multiple ventures during my business life, and yet if I had the chance to start all over again with half the knowledge that I currently have, I would do it in a heartbeat, without any hesitation. While it's impossible for me start again with the awareness and information that I now possess, I can share my experiences and understanding with eager immigrant entrepreneurs who are ready to learn and benefit from my long-term success and even from my mistakes!

I've discovered there are specific challenges that I was able to face and overcome during my professional life. I am an immigrant, and I am not perfect in English, my second language. However, that never discouraged or held me back from improving! Instead it pushed me forward and encouraged me to learn how to improve my communication skills, my speech, and to reduce my accent.

This book is meant to help immigrants who want start a new venture or continue successfully with an existing one. The purpose is to share my experiences—full of different variables, obstacles, and events—that you too may encounter on your way to personal, financial, and professional success.

There are many things I've learned about being successful that I wish I had known in the earlier stages of my profession. It would have been extremely beneficial to have a friend advise me, or a book to read about some of the hardships of immigrant business owners.

I know that as an immigrant, and someone who must often deal with a language barrier, it's hard for you to predict or even imagine the variety of challenges and complications you will face as you strive toward becoming an entrepreneur. It can be difficult to find proper instruction and advice about how to manage a business on a daily basis. I understand!

The information I provide is not legal advice or financial advice. It's a simple understanding of your struggles. It provides guidance from my experiences, from one immigrant entrepreneur to another. As they say, "it's not rocket science." This book is my modest contribution to help explain some of the hardships encountered by immigrant business owners just like you, and to offer remedies to avoid them.

We know that we must work hard to achieve wealth and success in life, particularly in the business world. As the saying goes, "no pain, no gain." No matter what country you're in, headaches in business are unavoidable. I will offer suggestions about how to minimize these headaches in America, and how to deal with them when they occur. My information is simple and understandable. I am not a professional writer; I am a business owner, an entrepreneur, and a man of new ventures. This book will be filled with my personal experiences, suggestions, and interesting facts.

We've all seen movies and read books about people with tattered clothes and holes in their shoes who arrive in the United States, and then they work their way to success, fortune, and fame. This book is not a "rags-to-riches" story of an immigrant's road from hardship to wealth. It is about problem solving, minimizing headaches, and setting priorities. I'll discuss obstacles that a new immigrant entrepreneur has to deal with, including rethinking old ideologies, preparing for culture shift, protecting assets, and seeking qualified legal and financial advisors. I'll provide information regarding the many different rules, regulations, and customs that a new immigrant business owner will have to adapt to and implement to achieve success.

Maintaining a positive attitude and acknowledging a mindset for exceptional customer service is important. These ideas might sound general and familiar, but it is crucial to stress and elaborate on these topics and many others. This foundation is essential to the life and the success of any business.

As I mentioned, this is not a scientific formula, but it is a lifetime of experience, filled with mistakes and achievements, that I want to share with you. I've encountered mistakes that have caused my business to lose millions of dollars! If there had been a resource or an advisor to help me, I would have avoided some of those mistakes and achieved success and wealth without so many headaches. If I had known some of the pitfalls that I might face as an immigrant starting a business, I would be in a more successful place now.

Of course, I learned from my mistakes, and I'm very grateful to be where I am in life. I'm pleased to offer my experiences for your consideration to help you build your success and prosperity. My primary goal in writing this book is for you to have a guide to help you through the unknown territory of entrepreneurship—a friend to share in the good times and the bad times, and a hand to shake when your journey is one of success and prosperity.

Part 1

Accepting a New Mindset

▶ | 1

The Story of a Typical Immigrant

It's time to disassemble the parts of the jigsaw puzzle, or perhaps to piece another one together, for I find that, having come to the end of my story, my life is just beginning. – Conrad Veidth

The Story of a Typical Immigrant

▶ | I've come a long way since my emigration from Lebanon to the United States in 1988. While this book isn't a memoir, you might be curious to know a little about my background, so you can recognize that I can relate to you and your dreams!

I want my experiences to show how I came to be in a position to assist other immigrants in their entrepreneurial quest. I want to help you realize that my true desire is to help people in the same position I was in, by sharing my ideas and the lessons I've learned throughout the course of many years.

Like many of the roughly one million immigrants who come to the United States each year and are granted permanent resident status, I'm a "typical" immigrant. At age eighteen I arrived in New York with little money and no family connections. I spoke no English and lived in a motel for the first few days. I found work as a cab driver before opening a small clothing store in uptown Manhattan. I attended LaGuardia Community College in Queens, New York before transferring to California State University, Long Beach, where in 1996 I graduated with bachelor of science degree in electrical engineering, biomedical and clinical engineering.

Even though my degree is in engineering, I spent many years working in sales. In this role, I used my scientific mindset and reasoning skills to adapt a new strategy to solve problems and fulfill the needs of others.

As the result of many years of hard work and dedication, I have become a successful businessman with a variety of ventures. I own an automotive dealership, invest in real estate, and operate several online companies. I have been blessed with a wonderful, supportive wife and four beautiful children. I've also become a naturalized U.S. citizen.

I'm extremely fortunate to be where I am right now. I empathize with those of you who are willing to work hard to be successful, and I relate to the possibility that you're feeling lost and don't know exactly what to do. You're probably getting advice from many people, and, unfortunately, it's likely the wrong advice from the wrong people. This is what I want to help you figure out.

As I mentioned in the introduction to this book, I wish I had known at the beginning of my career what I know now. Part of life is learning these lessons yourself; but to help other immigrant entrepreneurs avoid the pitfalls, I believe in passing down the ideas that I have learned.

You might have already started a business that's producing and things seem to be going well. But are you sure you have the right knowledge to make it through the maze of business strategies and decisions without getting lost on your path to success?

A perfect example of this is the financial aspect of a business venture. One of my most crucial mistakes was not being knowledgeable about financial matters. I unwisely took advice from a weak financial advisor regarding tax filing and proper fiscal planning. This error set back the potential growth my business by years. If I had known the things I do now, my current multimillion-dollar corporation would conservatively be worth five times what it is.

Today, I realize how important it is to secure the best financial advisor available, and to understand the significance of incorporating the business, filing taxes, preparing for an audit, and having the financial awareness to handle any situation that might arise. (More information on financial matters is discussed in Part 3, Preserve Wealth.)

By sharing some of my background with you, I hope you appreciate that I am on your side. I want to be your advocate and help you find your way through the maze of challenges that you will face. I am a typical immigrant who has become a successful entrepreneur. My goal is for you to be able to make this same statement with your business ventures.

► | 2

Rethink Old Ideologies

I always imagined a day when I would be my own boss. It was just a question of being persistent, trying out new ideas, and waiting for a breakthrough. – Alex Tew

▶ | It's exciting to start on a new venture. Actually, it's mind dazzling! All your ideas and dreams are put into reality. All you need to do is start implementing those ideas, those dreams, and those visions that you have been tossing around in your head during your sleepless nights. Today is the day to get started. Lots of hard thinking goes into the process, especially at the beginning.

Where do I start? How do I start? Once the first step is taken, everything starts falling into place. Things will become a little bit easier as your dream gets closer to being implemented. The process will begin to happen, and you will be happier, more enthusiastic, and more excited about the future as you progress toward fulfilling your goals.

Leaving your home and emigrating to a new country requires leaving nearly everything behind. That includes a preset mind that might be full of old ideologies, fears, and negative thoughts. Most of us immigrants come from a struggling background, where we lacked opportunities and had a poor quality of life.

Experiencing these mutual frustrations, we emigrated to the United States, seeking a better quality of life, success, and a great potential to generate wealth. We share the same dreams and visions. We're willing to work hard to achieve what we want. But too often we don't have a good plan or proper guidelines to fulfill our desires.

When coming to the United States, many immigrants bring with them a corrupt mindset that was generated through years of hardship. Most of the abuse came from governments that suppressed common people and pushed us down to the poverty line. A common way of thinking, which I grew up accepting, was, "The rich get richer, and the poor get poorer."

You're either way up in the upper class or you stay trapped in the lower class.

In many countries, corrupt businesses are the most successful. It's common to see an unethical business generating large profits. Many of us never dared to dream that there was room for a poor person to work hard and have an astonishing opportunity, and even to become a part of the upper class, successful community!

You need to believe that the United States really is different. Now that you are here, banish the mindset that you can't begin a new life and become a successful entrepreneur, even if you were considered a poor person in your previous country. If you continue with this preset mind, it makes it hard to believe that honest business ventures can lead to huge success and great wealth for you.

As you become attuned to a different culture (in your personal life and your business life), be ready and willing to adapt to new ways of viewing amazing opportunities for you and your family. You can still embrace the culture and traditions of your native country, but immigrants should not be afraid to leave behind old ways of thinking and discard any preset ideas of fear and corruption.

▶ | 3

Between Two Worlds

A nation's culture resides in the heart and in the souls of its people. – Mahatma Gandhi

► | When immigrants come to the United States, they arrive with their dreams, looking forward to the opportunity to put the obstacles from their previous country aside. They want to embrace their new country. However, most people still want to remember the good things about the people and the culture they left. I too wanted to maintain my cultural identity.

This dilemma is what I call "lost between the two worlds." You grew up in a country that is different from what you're facing now. Back home, there was a different culture, a different language, and maybe even a different religion. Holidays and family traditions might have been quite dissimilar from what you find in the new country. You and your family are suddenly faced with a new life and a completely different way of looking at everything.

It's as if you now have two brains. One of your brains is trying to grasp the American way, and the other brain takes you back to your roots and how you were raised. The old country where you grew up is familiar, comfortable, and easy to understand. You know this new country is where your dreams lie, and you also want to be comfortable here.

You might find times when you seem to be thinking with both brains, and you will have to struggle to silence the "old country" brain. You want to achieve your goals with the thinking of the "new country" brain. Especially in the beginning, it can be an everyday struggle, because you know you are reaching toward the benefits that come with new thinking, but you are also cautious, as there might also be a lot of downfalls.

Sometimes you have to just sit and analyze the struggle, and try to acknowledge the benefit of both worlds. It's not easy. I will give you an example that almost every immigrant faces. When you are learning a new language, it's extremely difficult to *think* in one language and *talk* in a different one.

I always tried to tell myself that if I had a thought in Arabic, I would not try to translate it into the English language, because if I became confused, then whoever was listening to what I was saying would become confused.

In the beginning, when you're going about your day-to-day life, you might have to force yourself to think of things in the American way. When you are at your business, talking to your employees, with vendors, and with other company leaders, it's important to display confidence that you are embracing your new life.

When you return to your home and your family, you want to revive that "inner you"—the you that was kept pressed down all day. You want to recapture that place of comfort when you go home. It's easy to go back to living in the old lifestyle, the old language, and the old traditions. I am here to tell you that you will eventually discover a balance between your old life and your new life, and you will not be lost between two worlds.

Of course, you want to raise your children with the knowledge of their heritage and teach them the values and traditions that you believe. I think it's the people who make this country great, and also what makes this country the strongest. Each individual who comes to this country tries to bring his or her best and transfer it into American life. It's one of the best assets that immigrants have to offer, and you should be proud to offer your unique input to the mix!

This topic of preparing for a culture shift is important. Every immigrant will experience the pull between going back and not going back. Knowing this, you can make every attempt to transition your business practices away from the old way of thinking. You want to adapt your creative innovations to the new way of doing business in the United States.

There might be rules and regulations that are different from what you learned in your previous country. Some ideas or customs might seem strange, compared to what you are accustomed to doing.

Remember that while certain business and social rules and customs are different, and you'll need to observe them, this does not mean that you need to abandon your *values*. Keep your values and beliefs, and use them to learn and grow, and adapt them to your new life.

► | 4

The American Way of Business

There is a powerful driving force inside every human being, that once unleashed can make any vision, dream, or desire a reality.

— Tony Robbins

▶ | In our home countries, in order to survive many business people make the rational choice to "play the game" with local politicians and other authorities. It's just something that you have to do in order to succeed in business. Upon coming to America, one issue that was difficult for me and many of my friends and business associates from foreign countries is leaving behind the idea that I can outsmart everybody else, or that I can use previous methods to beat the system. Perhaps at home I know a way to make that extra dollar that I'm not supposed to be making. This is where I learned that I could fall into a trap, and once I was in that trap, it took many years to recover.

Don't do it! You will find yourself suffering pain, having headaches, and losing sleep at night. You've wasted time and energy that should have been used focusing on the real issues, concentrating on the actual moneymaking product, and developing your business plans, which will allow you to grow.

Look at the pattern of many American corporations. They start with one small business, and they find a niche and expand each year. In perhaps a decade, they have grown into multiple locations, with multimillion-dollar profits. Often immigrant entrepreneurs will start a business and appear to be successful, but they think they can beat the system and don't always follow the rules. They have methods that might have been successful in their previous country, and they try to create a similar scheme in an attempt to outsmart the American system.

We think we are so smart, making that extra money, only later to wind up paying for it ten times over. When this happens, we lose the momentum and excitement we had in the beginning of our venture. The initial potential we anticipated is gone, and our business is ruined, often to the point of failure, or, at the very least, set back many years.

All those brilliant ideas you thought were so smart can damage your reputation and your investment. You might end up paying fines that are more than the extra money you made. Your emotional state can also suffer because of the error in judgment, so you end up paying for your mistake on many different levels.

Why do immigrants come to this country with the mentality of taking shortcuts to success? This is a common problem with some immigrants. Speaking from my own experience, I believe it is not that immigrants are trying to get around the system, but this is all they might have experienced or learned. In many underdeveloped countries, success to a few businesses comes with the help of bribery, from money laundering, and from bending the rules. Of course, this is generally speaking. This is not meant to discredit legitimate businesses.

In many other countries, it's expected that you need to make connections with certain government politicians and authorities so they can bend the rules to let you avoid taxation, permits, and inspections. Building wealth and being successful is based on this concept, and these owners are considered role models for establishing a business. Too often, the people in other countries who follow these methods are the ones who have the companies that are most successful, with the ability and the opportunity to demolish or beat the competition.

I'll give you an example of this mindset. Say there's an official who has discovered a fantastic deal on fire extinguishers through a certain supplier. He buys thousands of the fire extinguishers with plans to make a huge profit. He has an influence on the decision makers in the Ministry of Affairs or the Transportation Ministry and arranges to make a new law that states, "No cars are allowed to be on the road without a fire extinguisher." How convenient that he has thousands of fire extinguishers readily available for immediate purchase, because the consumer needs to follow the new law. Boom! He has just made millions!

This official might not even be business minded or an entrepreneur, and he's certainly unethical from a business standard practice. If you really are smart, you can create many schemes such as this, and in some countries it's considered business as usual.

These ideas are passed down through the generations, with the idea that this is the way you have to do business in order to be successful. You might see someone with a lot of money, whose company is quite fortunate, and then you realize the company owned by a government official or a person with many connections.

Corruption is everywhere in this world, but it's obvious that this person bent the rules and did something that wasn't supposed to be done. The message is sent to business owners that if they want to be rich and successful, they have to do the same things, because that is the easy way to generate wealth.

Another common misconception among new immigrants is the idea that making money is as easy as picking it off a tree. Someone has tricked people into thinking all you have to do is buy it, sell it, and you have a never-ending supply of money. No, it doesn't work like that!

There are invisible partners in your business, represented by different tax agencies, whether city, county, state, or federal. Also there are banks that front the funds to buy the products. Businesses must follow their rules and meet their increasing demands. Otherwise, they will suffer a great deal of stress and financial burden.

Please believe that there's no such thing as "easy money." There is money that's earned, that's come from hard work and planning. You might think certain people are lucky, because they seem to make money much faster than other people do. It's a lucky break, so to speak. If you observe their work habits, you will find that they put a lot of time, energy, and hard work into their ventures. We are all inclined to look for lucky breaks and great fortune. Or we can just believe the saying, "People make their own luck."

You have to make wise choices when you are deciding what you want to do. Money does not grow on trees. You have to do it the right way by working hard and learning ways to save and invest your earnings.

▶ | 5

The Customer Relationship

There exist limitless opportunities in every industry. Where there is an open mind, there will always be a frontier. – Charles F. Kettering

► | According to many immigrants' experiences, it's refreshing to know that most of us walk into American businesses with an open mind. Trusting that the salesperson is telling us the truth about the product, we accept the presentations with faith and confidence in the establishment. In turn, the business owners also need to be open minded, accepting remarks and criticisms without becoming defensive. Valuing your customer is essential, and you should always believe that people are being honest with their comments. You don't want to view customers' comments as not being truthful.

It is important to believe that the consumer is *usually* right; approaching every customer with this in mind will result in excellent customer satisfaction ratings. Most consumers are accustomed to being pampered and treated with respect and dignity, which is as it should be. Some consumers might be challenging, and you must have an open mind in dealing with these clients. In the majority of situations, you should accept that they are being truthful in their interactions with you.

If you have doubts that they are not being honest, you should handle it delicately and try not to be confrontational. It's best to try to follow the motto that your customers are right. Even when they're wrong, they still have the power to affect your business!

Operating a business and producing sales must come with extraordinary standards, especially for the immigrant entrepreneur. It's important to maintain a high level of dignity and righteousness. We must take into consideration that most customer complaints wind up being in the favor of the customer. Even when a dispute ends up in the court system or is reported to the Better Business Bureau, mediators always encourage the business involved to attempt to fulfill the customer's needs. This helps maintain the reputation of an honest business.

Most of the time, customer satisfaction can be achieved by keeping your mind open, accepting complaints with a positive attitude, and compromising, if necessary. Your optimistic approach will lead to better reviews of your business and a higher customer satisfaction rating.

There are several online sites, such as Angie's List and Yelp, which allow customers to provide feedback and ratings about their experiences with service providers and businesses. You don't want to have a low rating or negative comments on a website that thousands of potential customers might view!

Throughout my years of customer interaction, I've learned that there might be times, from your first contact, when you recognize a particularly difficult customer. You might consider the need to filter these customers and try not to encourage a sale! Although it might seem a bit harsh, this is called "firing the customer."

What do I mean by this phrase? It's simply refusing to engage in business with people who begin their approach with a bad attitude. You have a sense that they are going to be impossible to please. Many of these people are time bombs waiting to explode. They could have been "burned" by another business or perhaps they might have some mental health issues. Regardless of the reason, they are trouble waiting to happen. A simple way of saying this is that there are some people in the market place who are "hard to deal with." I recommend not doing business with them.

It's been my experience that you cannot really satisfy people with this type of personality. If you try to, most of the time the interaction will consume too much of your time, energy, and resources. In the end, the damage to your business and your reputation is irreparable, and might even be expensive. If customers are argumentative and give you a hard time at the beginning of the transaction, even before the sale is conducted, imagine what complaints they're going to come back with later.

As the very wise Imam Ali Ibn Abi Talib said, "The moment you start arguing with an ignorant person, you have already lost."

In business words, the moment you start arguing with a customer, you've already lost the sale. Your business should attempt to serve every customer to meet their needs and wants to the best of your ability. As much as you would like to, it's impossible to satisfy one hundred percent of the people who walk through your door. Remember the idea of filtering customers, to ensure you work with the right ones for your business, and don't waste your time on the wrong ones. It's not always predictable, but follow your gut instinct!

If you have a bad feeling about a particular person or transaction, back away and avoid trouble. Throughout the years, I have been able to say, "No more." I don't want to be the type of salesperson who feels like he has to force the customer to buy simply to say, "I got a sale." If a customer comes back with a complaint about the product or begins to criticize my business or me, I promptly reimburse them or reverse the transaction; or, to make the matter simple and clear, I just refund the money.

Sometimes it's best to just let it go in an effort to maintain a good customer relationship. Even losing a sale can turn out for the best, because we have provided satisfaction to the customer. In the end, it probably saved a lot of time, money, and the headache of dealing with a person who wasn't happy.

Always keep an open mind when you are interacting with people. Even your employees and coworkers deserve the benefit of the doubt. When you have confidence and your mind is free to accept new ideas, new customers will open the door to further success!

► | 6

Get Experience Before You Launch Your Own Business

No matter how many mistakes you make or how slow you progress, you are still way ahead of everyone who isn't trying.

– Tony Robbins

Get Experience Before You Launch Your Own Business

▶ | I've been asked what I would recommend to new immigrants regarding their careers. Should they get a job with the skills they already possess, or should they begin their new life with their own business? This situation requires consideration about the kind of person you are, your resources, and the degree of your ambition. Most of all it demands a firm understanding of the culture, customs, and language of your new country.

I've always had a spirit of entrepreneurship. I never had a job working for someone else, and yet it's difficult for me to suggest that is the best way for you to go. Let me offer this idea: Think about where you see yourself, how you want to interact with your skills, and how you envision your life.

If I were to go back to 1988, to when I first arrived in the United States, I would get a job in the field that I would like to invest in for the future. I would use that job to learn what I needed to know; I'd learn from my mistakes and grow to the level that I could open my own business in two or three years.

I would learn from my experiences, the positive and the negative, and I would gather all these thoughts and organize a business plan. Working for someone else, I could save money and be able to launch my own business—stronger, smarter, and with much more confidence than if I had started without any experience.

As an immigrant entrepreneur, I learned the ups and downs of business with my own money. It would have been easier if I had educated myself by being an employee in a good business and having somebody pay me while they helped me hone my skills and gain confidence. I could have practiced my profession, learned how to plan business strategies, and had the opportunity to observe my coworker's methods for dealing with situations.

As an immigrant, it's important to get to know your way around your new surroundings and embrace your life in your new country. While you are working for someone else, develop a grasp of the English language. You can practice with your coworkers and with customers. Use every opportunity to improve your knowledge of the business you wish to pursue. When you are ready, you can gather your contacts, and be prepared to launch your own business on a strong foundation.

Instead of wasting my money and my time on my own, trying to learn all aspects (from small to large) of a business, I would be able to pick up on the small issues by working for someone else. That way I would have a chance to observe people dealing with issues, and I'd be better prepared when it was my turn! That's why I recommend that most people, whatever field they have experience in, work for someone else for a while, until they are acclimated to life in the United States.

For example, let's say there is a chef who owned a successful restaurant in Lebanon. He diligently saved his money to open a restaurant in the United States. The Lebanese chef found a home in America and opened his restaurant. He spent a lot of money on the building, interior decorating, equipment, and supplies. He did everything here that he did for his successful business in Lebanon. But he finds that he is failing in his American venture and the business might not survive a year or two.

Our Lebanese chef arrived in the United States with his hard-earned money and immediately jumped into a new business. He definitely possessed the knowledge to run a restaurant, but he didn't know how to deal with his new life and its culture, social mandates, laws, environmental requirements, permits, consumer actions, inspections, rules, and regulations. He didn't have time to learn how to play by the rules.

He doesn't want to waste the money he's invested, so he's faced with the struggle of trying to outsmart the system. He's blindsided by the number of issues he knew nothing about. He's plagued with problems and headaches that will not go away because he doesn't know how to fix them. He's starting to lose his inspiration and has begun to make mistakes.

If government agencies are misunderstood, he might have serious legal trouble. Local, state, and national regulations can be a nightmare to a natural citizen. You can't imagine the terror of immigrants when they have to deal with authorities on complex issues including taxation, worker's compensation, unemployment, food inspection, toxic products, water conservation, safety regulations—the list is mind boggling.

The reason why this immigrant entrepreneur failed is that he never gave himself the opportunity to learn and adapt to the cultural changes. He needed time to become familiar with the language, learn the new rules, new regulations, and new ways of interacting with his customers. If this man had started his career in the United States as a chef, an assistant, or perhaps a restaurant manager, after two or three years he would have said, "Oh, I see now! This is how to deal with this person," or "Oh, that's what he meant," or "Now I understand the proper answer when somebody complains."

The new experiences would have shown our chef that business practices in the United States might be completely different from those in Lebanon. After a few years, he would have been fully prepared to launch his own business. His time had been well spent learning the language, interacting with coworkers and customers, gaining knowledge about products, obtaining legal and financial advisors—and, *boom*, he'd be a success!

Consider the different customs from various countries that send emigrants to the United States. Perhaps in one country the people do not typically say "please," and it's perfectly acceptable there to not say it. Now I'm in a country where saying "please" is expected, and if it's not said, it is considered bad manners or rude. Of course, as a new immigrant, I'm not used to saying it, and I'm losing a lot of business because of that mistake.

Here's another example. If I have not allowed myself time to speak and understand English, I might erroneously translate a sentence from my language to English, and it might offend someone. A word might be misinterpreted and the wrong message sent. Any innocent errors will cause a loss of customers and contribute to business failure. People might appreciate the spirit of enthusiasm about your business, but if they can't communicate with you without running the risk of being misunderstood, they will go somewhere else.

Mistakes can be costly, both in terms of financial loss and in emotional well being. Take these examples and learn from the mistakes of others who have gone before you, so you can avoid wasted time, energy, and money.

► | 7

A Positive Attitude Boosts Your Bottom Line

Do not learn how to react; learn how to respond. – Buddha

▶ | Expressing ourselves in a professional way requires a lot of practice and patience. The proper words, said at the right time, might bring wealth, while the wrong words can bring ruin.

We are human. We all have our ups and downs. Sometimes I wake up in the morning and I just don't feel like going to work. I have my issues—personal, relationship, and all sorts and kinds of financial responsibilities and obligations—but I still have to work.

The bottom line is even though I might not be in a good mood, I still have to show up to work and perform to the best of my ability. I enter the workplace with a smile and a happy voice, greeting all the staff and everybody else around me, and receiving greetings in return. I'd like to believe that I'm someone who is enjoyable to be around. It sets the tone of the day for all of us!

My personal issues are my own. They are no one else's business. I need to act as if I have full strength and energy. In other words, if necessary, as long as I'm physically in the office, I *pretend* to be in a great mood, or simply happy to be there, where I am needed most. Even though I'm not really feeling it one hundred percent, that energy and happiness reflect on the productivity of my coworkers, my employees, my staff, and, most important, of myself.

It's essential to maintain that type of attitude, not only to be able to generate energy and happiness around the workplace, but also to create a trend. If you do this every day, and it's a consistent habit, the other employees and associates will get used to and expect it. They begin to see you as someone who enjoys life and is good to be around. It helps them adapt the same kind of energy and happiness to their life, which translates to happy customers and increased sales.

The employees see what the leader is capable of and what we are doing. The leader is the role model, and employees will try to act the same way. Our energy and attitude reflects on them. What if I come to work with an angry, sad, or downturned face? What kind of atmosphere would I generate? Everybody, including the staff and associates, would have to stay away from me—the person who is their leader, the boss, and the owner of the business. This can only hurt the business. And it did, in my case! From my own experience, I learned this the hard way. My attitude, whether negative or positive, reflects directly on how everybody else around me performs.

Why Should We Have a Positive Attitude?

The advantage of coming to work with a positive attitude, happiness, and a smile on your face is that you can energize your staff. A simple smile and eye contact will energize employees and create a positive energy around the whole business, which leads to more productivity. This is important because productivity generates sales, and, as we all know, businesses are based on sales.

So to review, that positive attitude combined with happiness is going to generate more sales for the business. And if you come to work with a positive attitude, you'll discover that it's easier to deal with the obstacles and hardships that might happen throughout the day. Your reaction to the daily challenges will be calmer and more professional. You'll also find that the consequences are always easier.

Generally speaking, a positive attitude produces positive communication, because the attitude that you have deep inside you is reflected by your communications. Positive interactions and communication tell the staff that the leadership is full of life. The staff, employees, and other people around you will admire your vigorous, active, and electrified energy.

Throughout my years of being in a leadership position, I have found it extremely helpful to advise the staff to leave their problems behind when they come to work. They can talk about personal issues on their personal time. It's imperative for the team members to leave their negative attitude and the contagious influence it has at home or where they encountered it.

They should come to work with a positive attitude, intent on changing the negative! They can say,

> "I want to go to work. I want to generate income and money and improve my life. So I'm going there with a happy, positive attitude. I want my coworkers and my customers to find me enjoyable to be around.

> "I'm going to leave my problems at home and solve them later. The influence and the charge of positive energy that I receive at work will go home with me and help me to solve my problems."

A positive attitude is a choice. What is not a choice for a company or a business is generating income. You cannot motivate and successfully lead people with a negative attitude. Therefore, a positive attitude is essential. It's monumental to move people in a direction of profit or the direction you want them to go.

To preserve the positive culture that it took you years and years to create, sometimes people with negative attitudes in your organization have to be strategically removed from the company. A person with a negative attitude is like cancer in the body. It will destroy the organization from the inside out. This way of looking at life is a contagious negativism that has no place in your successful business.

To be a leader who is positive and helps create happiness and good energy, here are some things that you can say to your associates and your staff that will inspire them and give them motivation and a great positive attitude to continue to do their best for you!

- Whatever you set your mind to, you can achieve.

- I succeeded by never offering or accepting any excuses.

- We become what we imagine and strive for.

- Either you control your life, or your life controls you.

- Dream your future—and then start to work on it.

- Your vision needs power, genius, and imagination.

- If you believe you can reach your goal, you're halfway there.

- The highest walls are constructed in our minds.

- Only with imagination will our possibilities be limitless.

► | 8

Don't Beat the System—Master the System

You have to learn the rules of the game. And then you have to play better than anyone else. – Albert Einstein

► | Within every business venture, there are systems and boundaries. These are the foundations for operating a legal, ethical enterprise. There are established guidelines, rules, regulations, permits, and obligations every business owner must fulfill in order to have a functioning business. Without this foundation, a business might initially succeed, if the owner is highly motivated and the product or services he is selling are exceptional. However, there will eventually come a time in every business when an owner will discover that attempting to ignore or sidestep one of these fundamental obligations will cause the business to fail.

Certainly, there are methods by which one could attempt to beat the system by trying to outsmart it, or do something illegal or unethical to avoid one's obligations. Allowing these maneuvers would only be a temporary fix to a problem that will surely resurface later. Circumventing a required business responsibility will lead to unnecessary problems and headaches in the future. You could face legal action or costly fines, and when certain laws and required systems are not met your business could even be shut down. In addition to legal penalties, your business could suffer from media exposure for not following the regulations, thereby projecting a bad image to your customers, whom you've worked so hard to get.

As an ethical person, I would never suggest any method for avoiding the rules or the boundaries of the system. They are there to create a level playing field for everyone, and it wouldn't be fair if some were allowed to evade the rules, regardless of the ability to do so. For example, an unethical contractor might suggest that he can build an addition to your business without obtaining the required permits or paying the necessary fees. He might also suggest extra payment to him for saving you the permit fee and the extra time avoided in the building process.

Not only have you sidestepped the law, which could bring a penalty, but you are in a position of being blackmailed by the contractor in the future. Moreover, if something happens and the new building addition contributes to someone being hurt, you don't have any legal recourse against the contractor. You are simply asking for trouble if you choose to ignore the systems that are there to protect everyone.

Don't try to beat the system—become the master of the system. Every entrepreneur needs to do their homework and learn the applicable local, state, and federal laws and regulations in depth, so you have complete knowledge and understanding of every regulation that is required for your business. Become familiar with the system, adapt to it, and always operate within the boundaries. It might seem overwhelming to learn these rules, but it will save you headaches in the end.

Depending on the type of business you intend to operate, you need to know the time limits involved in securing an initial permit or license, how often it needs to be renewed, and when to expect periodic inspections. Know the building codes and fire codes for your city, county, state, and even the federal requirements. Learn everything you can about hiring (and firing) employees and other human resource requirements. If you offer a service that involves food, there are many regulations that you must follow to operate safely within the boundaries of restaurant guidelines.

Most important, know whom to call if you have questions! People who have lived in the United States for a long time don't always know these systems. As an immigrant, you can master the system by learning everything you need to know to avoid problems. Ask successful businesspeople and they will tell you that they learned the system and adapted to it. The only way to master the system is to play within its boundaries and observe the rules and regulations.

This is not a new revelation that I have just discovered. Sometimes simply following the rules makes the most sense. People succumb to their human nature to try to find an easier, quicker way to do things. They might not stop to consider that the idea of becoming knowledgeable is the best way to master the system.

As an immigrant, when I came to my new country and wanted to start my own business, some of my greatest challenges included learning how to deal with this complicated system. All the rules and regulations can be extremely complex and frustrating, especially if the rules are nothing like the methods you dealt with in your old country. This is not an excuse you can allow yourself to consider!

As an immigrant, there will be some customs and traditions from your previous country that you can incorporate in your new business, such as decorating, music, and exceptional customer service. When it comes to following the laws of your new country, you need to get rid of the old mentality of what was acceptable in the past. Embrace the new mentality that American businesses demand.

► | 9

Never Stop Learning

Seek knowledge from the cradle to the grave.

– Prophet Muhammad

▶ | An open-minded successful business owner listens, tries new things, and reflects honestly on success and failures. Success in business does not require a master's degree or a doctorate. Amazingly, some immigrant entrepreneurs behave in these ways today. Mostly it's when they reach the age of thirty-five and, specifically, if they reach their goals and experience success.

Let's move ahead a few years. At last you have found your niche, and you're in the business where you feel you should be. As a fellow immigrant entrepreneur, I can relate to your excitement and the achievements you have made so far. It might be tempting to be satisfied that you have reached this goal and begin to relax in your venture.

However, this is the time that you need to continue learning, because your business is evolving, and it can change so rapidly that sometimes it's hard to keep up the momentum. That's why you should never stop learning! You need to stay up to date on everything pertaining to your specific line of work.

As you grow, always keep things in perspective, stay on top of current trends, and keep in touch with new methods and technologies available to benefit your business. Follow proper management procedures and learn as much as you can about anything new that will assist in the advancement of your business.

When you're providing a product for sale or a service to your customers, you need to know the latest updates on the market trends. You need to have the newest version of whatever is available; otherwise, the price will be driven down and your competition might gain the upper hand.

You have to be one of the first to grab the opportunities as soon as they become available, so you will be up to date with any changes or improvements to your market. When you have the reputation for being "in the know" about the newest trends and products, you'll gain the respect of your customers and even your competitors.

When I started my business in the late 1980s, most of the marketing we did was focused in newspapers, magazines, and other paper advertising. We did no online internet promotions because the internet was not really utilized then. After a few years, our advertising techniques shifted to include radio and television. We often searched for a high-traffic area to display our business on billboards.

In only a few years, our marketing programs have completely changed. Today we do no paper advertising and almost everything is done via internet advertising.

If we had stuck with what worked in the 1980s, we would have been out of business a long time ago. It's important to keep up with the changes that are happening in the world, to keep generating sales and creating leads. Most of our business transactions are done through reaching customers online or advertising online. Online is a powerful resource, and it provides a new business the opportunity to reach a large audience with a limited advertising budget.

The need for a huge marketing budget is not as vital as it was when paper advertisements, billboards, and radio ads were popular. In recent years, smart phone apps have become popular, and this is growing advertising method that you might want to research for your specific business product.

Regardless of the type of business that you own, stay on top of the current trends for all aspects of your enterprise. In the past few years, airwave operation rules involving television, cable, and Wi-Fi have changed. Licensing laws, labor regulations, and human resource requirements are frequently modified. Keep informed about the latest legal and financial information to protect your investment.

Continuing education for management skills and customer service expertise is a good investment for anyone in your business who deals directly with customers. The bottom line is, "Never stop learning!" Knowledge is power, and you will have the confidence to know that you are doing everything possible to benefit your business and its continued success.

► | 10

Connect with Like-Minded People

Surround yourself with positive people. Surround yourself with only people who are going to lift you higher. – Oprah Winfrey

► | As an immigrant in business, it's important to connect with like-minded people and to network with other individuals who share your same ideals, goals, and enthusiasm. When we meet with these people, we're able to pick up business from other sources and identify people who might need our services. That, in turns, leads to more money and future opportunities for our businesses. You might find business associates whom you respect and with whom you can compare thoughts and ideas. Because you're connected by a common interest, they might be aware of a new opportunity that they are happy to share with you,.

Another reason to connect with people with the same interests is that it helps you stay fresh. Entrepreneurs have a different way of thinking, and we are often misunderstood. When I talk to other entrepreneurs, I understand the way they think and how they talk, because it's almost identical to the way I think and how I talk. I've noticed this common personality trait in many entrepreneurs.

Sometimes our families don't understand what we do or the way our mind works. They cannot relate to our business, our stress, our job, and what happens at the office. When we talk to other entrepreneurs, we can release some of that stress by being heard and understood. Many times we can feel we are being guided or mentored by people who have been in our situations. Connecting with like-minded people helps us maintain our enthusiasm for our work, and knowing we have other people who understand our thought process is valuable.

How do we locate people who share this common bond? One of the easiest, most convenient places to find individuals and groups is by going online. You can join Facebook groups and find individuals who share your interests. You can go to www.meetup.com and join groups. Then you have the opportunity to meet these people online and in real life. Ideally, I recommend that you connect with people in person, and not only through your computer screen.

Many trade organizations have workshops, conventions, and events. Find listings for similar businesses, and contact the owner or manager to find out what offerings are available in your area. Civic organizations are another great place to meet like-minded people. When you attend events or meetings, always have plenty of your personal business cards, because you're going to meet many people who are eager for new information that can make them better entrepreneurs.

Mastermind groups are another online resource to find connections with like-minded people. Some of the options are free and some charge a fee, but it's nominal compared to the quality connections you will make. LinkedIn is not as social as other suggestions I've listed, but it does provide connections with other professional people.

Perhaps you aren't the most social person in the world, but it will only be to your advantage to make connections with other people—both immigrant and native—who share the same goals and dreams. Knowing you have a friend in the business is a great gift when you need someone reliable to share the ups and downs of your life!

► | 11

Develop Your Leadership Skills

Before you can get others to believe, you have to believe.

▶ | The journey to leadership is an inner quest to discover who you are. Leadership is self-development. Through your self-development comes the confidence to lead. What this is all about is awareness and belief in your own strength and power.

As you begin the journey toward leadership, you must face challenges and difficulties. Some of these difficulties are: having a clear vision, knowing your exact values, and finding what gives you the courage to continue in the face of uncertainty.

Ask yourself:

• What are my strengths?

• What are my weaknesses?

• What keeps me motivated?

• How do I become more encouraged?

• How do I encourage my team?

When mistakes are made, leaders don't look for someone to blame. But these questions rise to the surface: "What can I learn from these mistakes? How can I turn my mistakes into experience and try to avoid them happening again?"

The challenge is to keep long-term success, and your long-term vision, in mind and at the forefront of your actions. Although it is often necessary to achieve a fast and immediate win, leaders can identify the place from where they can start. This will help you make the project seem accessible and doable, within the existing skills and available resources.

As a leader, you need to start the activity and proceed nonstop. Leaders begin with actions that are within their control—that are tangible, that are doable. They understand how hard it is to get somebody excited about just a dream or just a new venture. They know that they must show some kind of excitement and enthusiasm, and be optimistic about the future.

Absolute dedication to the business is necessary to set an example to others and to your employees. I cannot remember a time when I could separate my business life from my personal. I lived for the business and whatever the business needed. I was there 24/7, just like being married to it. This might sounds strange, but any entrepreneur will understand the way I felt, and the reason behind it.

It's important to recognize that without the leader (you), there would be no business. You set the standards for the way the business is operated. The standards you set for your personal life should be set the same way for the business. You are the certainty in the uncertain times. The business depends on your leadership and your skills.

When there is hardship or a challenge, you are the one to face it, pay the price, and deal with the problems, because you are the heart of the business. Your team counts on you, and any aspect of the business comes back to you. You hired the members of your team, you answer their questions, you assigned duties, and you are their leader.

When my business was smaller, I remember being involved in every single little detail of that business, and I was happy to do it. I had all the time and energy to focus on that. As my business grew and the duties multiplied, more professionals were added, and I was not always directly involved in the little details. However, I've never lost touch with any aspect of the business, and all my employees know they can count on me.

In order to be a good leader, you need to develop your leadership skills. There are many books and classes that will assist you with fine-tuning your skills. As with the other areas of your business, you need to always look for ways to improve your relationship with your staff. When you are constantly searching for ways to become better, you *will* become better, and the business will benefit from your efforts. Remember, the business is you, and you are the business. As you become more knowledgeable about your business, this is passed on to your team members, and the business will continue to grow and become more productive.

Communication with your staff is crucial. Listen to your employees as individuals and as a team. You've most likely been careful in your selection of hiring good people. Trust them and know that you are all working toward the same goal. It is important to accept their suggestions and their feedback. You will all benefit from sharing your thoughts and ideas, and you can learn from any mistakes that have been made.

Don't ever let your ego get in the way. You are the leader, and sometimes it might be easy to fall back on that fact. You might feel that whatever you do is above reproach. Face up to your problems and your mistakes. Your team will respect you for being human.

A great leader turns a negative challenge to a positive result by being willing to change and adapt. It's beneficial to have a mentor, or a fellow entrepreneur, you can trust to assist you with your challenges. Every business owner, large or small, needs to have someone to share with and to ask for opinions and advice. Ask for directions even if you know the way. Make sure to seek as many different expert opinions about a difficult or unfamiliar situation. There is nothing embarrassing about doing this.

Always keep your promises to your team members. They have faith and trust in you and will lose that if they see you are not a person of your word. If you fail on your commitment to them, they might begin to distrust you, hide things that happen, and not believe the things you tell them.

Try to implement an open-door policy, where employees feel welcome to come to you with problems or concerns. If you need to reprimand an employee, always make sure to do it in a private setting. Most people do not resent an error or lapse in judgment being addressed, but to do it in front of other people can cause embarrassment and ridicule. If you need to formally reprimand an employee, be sure you follow human resources best practices, and have the employee sign the record of the reprimand.

Don't be hesitant to get in there and work with your team. You might have reached the status where you no longer have to be at the front line of the store, but if you show your team members that you are always willing to be there for them, you will win their admiration. A good leader never forgets what it's like to be on the front line!

Be accountable for your mistakes. If you share your mistakes with your team members, they will know that you relate to their need to strive to become better. Good leaders will never deny or hide their mistakes, but use them as learning opportunities for everyone. You want to be the kind of leader who shares both the mistakes and the success stories. You don't want to only focus on where you were lacking, but also where you achieved! Praising your staff for a job well done provides the opportunity to make sure everyone feels that they are a part of the success.

If you are the least bit doubtful about your abilities to be a good leader, make a concerted effort to discover ways you can improve. As stated above, read books on the subject, take classes, or confide in a friend or fellow entrepreneur to give you advice and tips about what works for them.

You might consider hiring a life coach to help you recognize your strengths and weaknesses. You don't want to demand respect from your employees simply because you are the owner and in charge of the business. You want to *earn* respect, thus ensuring your success as a good leader.

Above all, a trusty motto to follow is this: "Treat others as you want to be treated."

Advantages and Disadvantages of Being a Business Owner

Opportunities are usually disguised as hard work, so most people don't recognize them. – Ann Landers

► | Being your own employer can be extremely rewarding. Owning a successful business is part of the American dream, and probably one of the primary reasons many people immigrate to this country.

As the owner of your business, you will gain a sense of independence, pride, and the self-confidence that you earn from your hard work. You will earn the respect of your stakeholders, who are the people connected to your business including your team, your business associates, your investors, and your customers. You will be a contributing asset to your community and your industry. As you glean the financial rewards of your success, you will also benefit from the personal satisfaction that being your own employer brings to your life.

Being the leader of your team, you will be involved in every aspect of the business operation. The first few years of your venture will be a learning process. There will be opportunities to acquire specific and general knowledge in the facets of the business that need more expertise. While you become more familiar with all areas of your business, as the team leader, you will be responsible for implementing your skills and knowledge and teaching your staff the proper methods you want utilized in your business. It is an awesome feeling to become an instructor or a "professor" of your field.

Successful leaders know all about their business. They are in direct contact with suppliers, attend to customers' needs, keep financial records, and know their inventory. You will have the pleasure to know that your staff members will depend on your skill and direction. It's important to remember that you are the model they will emulate. It's honorable to accept your position as head of the business. Having a positive attitude and a willingness to learn and work hard gives you great leverage, and the example you set will be the one they follow.

There are many advantages and disadvantages to owning your own business. Not everyone has the ability to adapt to the changes that will occur when you commit yourself to the hard work and time demands required. You need to be prepared for the challenges, sacrifices, and benefits that will transform your lifestyle.

Just as it is in your personal life, there will be ups and downs in your business life—good days and bad days. Being your own employer comes with many different kinds of risks. Financial risk is a huge factor, and it's important that you make wise decisions regarding your investment.

Another important risk factor is time. There will be occasions when it seems that you have all the time in the world, and then you suddenly feel as though you're running out of time. Time is money, but time has no tangible value for the business owner.

As the leader of your business, you will likely work twelve to fifteen hours every day, seven days a week, 365 days a year. Three-fourths of business owners work more than fifty hours per week. That's just a fact of life!

In the beginning of your business endeavor, the main contribution you can give is your time. As you wait for the customers to come and your business to grow, time seems to be one thing you have plenty of, and it doesn't cost you anything. However, having too much time on your hands can be stressful.

One of the most detrimental factors in owning your own business is the day-to-day stress you will experience. Issues can arise with employees, taxes, permits, vendors, losses, and other factors.

Many business headaches are the source of stress, and stress can be reduced by being proactive. It's best to address any problems as soon as possible, to minimize the damage, eliminate the issue, and reduce further stress in your life. It's important to remain energetic and maintain a positive example for your team to follow.

You should always be cognizant of creating a balance in your life. Be aware that there will be good times and bad times, and accept that reality as part of doing business. Prepare yourself for the lean times, such as when the economy is not good or an unforeseen obstacle occurs. Use your entrepreneurial spirit to discover new and creative methods to generate wealth. When you are able to endure the trials that might come your way, you will become stronger. You've gained valuable experience to make your business a success for many years to come.

My intention is not to discourage any entrepreneur who is planning to start a new venture. My aim is to create awareness of the advantages and disadvantages that will occur with entrepreneurship. I also want to shed light on a few important things, such as the potential risk of losing your life savings, or the chance of defaulting on loans that you've made to start your business. You will not have the comfort of a guaranteed income, as you would if you were an employee at another business.

On the other hand, you will enjoy the autonomy of owning your own business: when you own your own business, there's no boss who can fire you or lay you off to satisfy some larger corporate agenda. You'll learn to pay the bills on time, perform undesired but necessary duties, and manage a staff.

These are challenging tasks. People think that owning your own business allows you the freedom to enjoy your family and take vacations. While this can happen after many years of your hard work, and owning a business is gratifying in many ways, it can also be a tremendous burden when things don't run as smoothly as you had envisioned.

Despite some of the challenging aspects I've mentioned, I believe that owning your own business, and being your own boss, comes with many positive advantages that vastly outweigh the negative traits. If you possess a passion and desire to be your own employer, as I did, then you have the spirit that is necessary to meet the challenges of building a successful business.

Immigrant entrepreneurs just like you face challenges in reaching their dreams, but you can reach your goals with the knowledge and advice you receive from others who want to help you succeed. My purpose in acknowledging the advantages and disadvantages comes from years of experience, which resulted in ultimate success. I am honored to share some of my overwhelming experiences and strategies to assist you on your journey to be successful.

Part 2

Create Wealth

► | 13

How to Create Wealth

I refuse to feel guilty. I feel guilty about too much in my life but not about money. I went through periods when I had nothing, so somebody in my family has to get stinkin' wealthy.– Jim Carrey

► | The question of how to build wealth in the United States has been asked and answered hundreds of times, and most people already know that the answer is "hard work." If you work hard, it will pay off and you will become rich. This has been proven by many successful immigrant entrepreneurs including Sergey Brin, a Russian emigrant, who co-founded Google; Andrew Grove, originally from Hungary, who co-founded Intel; and both Steve Chen of YouTube and Jerry Yang of Yahoo came to the U.S. from Taiwan.

Some immigrants have become so much a part of the American landscape that we forget that they arrived in America with little but the money in their pocket. A good example is Arnold Schwarzenegger, who was born in Thal, Austria. He came to America in 1968 at the age of twenty-one. He was a successful bodybuilder who leveraged his ambition and hard work to become a huge Hollywood movie star and eventually the governor of California. Could he have run for president? Unfortunately, to become president of the United States you need to be native born. But you can become a U.S. senator, like Ted Cruz, who was born in Canada; to run for the U.S. Senate you need to have been a naturalized U.S. citizen for a period of at least nine years.

Thinking outside the box and daring to explore in new directions and modern technologies often leads to massive wealth. Even on a smaller level, when entrepreneurs find an untapped niche, they are likely to corner the market on their ideas and soon be wealthy.

We know that we have to work hard and earn money, but exactly how do we build wealth? I'm not talking about becoming a multimillionaire overnight, because that rarely happens. Most individuals simply want to have enough money to be comfortable and not have to worry about how they can support their families and enjoy a decent lifestyle. I think this is the typical scenario for an immigrant who just arrived in the United States. We left our previous country to find a better life, and we're starting here from nothing.

Hard work is the key to making money, and almost any eager person can find a job and make money. The idea of creating wealth is how you use that money after you've made it! You must have a plan and be wise as you venture into your own business, to have your savings work for you through smart planning and implementation. As stated earlier, in Part 1, in order to be successful and protect your investment, you must first learn the rules and boundaries, and then you must be committed to follow them.

Once you have established the required foundation, you must work constantly to manage your business. You will need the assistance of a professional financial advisor to help you protect your investments. Find someone who has worked with strong financial corporations, to ensure that he or she has the knowledge and the enthusiasm to help you create the wealth you want.

It is rewarding and beneficial to hire a professional accountant when you're beginning your business. You need to consider that it is a part of the foundation of your business, and if you don't support the foundation from all sides, it has the potential to crumble. Having an advisor is essential to make sure you have a wise plan for your accounting, taxes, audits, and other financial issues. This is just as important as following the laws regarding every aspect of the rules and boundaries.

You can't leave out any of the puzzle pieces and hope to have a complete picture. You have to use all the pieces to make it fit. It's highly unlikely you will create wealth overnight, but if you are patient and make it a part of your planning from the beginning, you will realize the wealth you are seeking.

▶ | 14

Your Customers Write Your Paycheck

We asked ourselves what we wanted this company to stand for. We didn't want to just sell shoes. I wasn't even into shoes—but I was passionate about customer service. – Tony Hsieh

▶ | Customer service is a relationship that develops between a company and a customer. Obviously, we want that relationship to be the best possible. Why is customer service important? Good customer service creates sales, and sales are the essential component of every business. In a very real sense, your paycheck is written not by you, but by your customers.

If our customers experience bad service, they won't want to buy our products. They will go to an establishment where they are given attention and treated with respect, even if they might end up paying more for the same product.

Customer service plays a part in every aspect of your business. Good relationships are the foundation of business, from the vendors you use to obtain your product, to the salesperson who sells it. This service even continues after the sale is generated. The person who answers the phone requires positive customer service skills and is as important as the person conducting the transaction, whether it is in sales, service, or other areas of your business.

If customers are happy with the service they receive at your business, they will pass that word on to friends and neighbors. They might even go online and write a good review about it on consumer websites, such as Google Review or Yelp.

Either by word of mouth or online, good reviews will ultimately lead to new and repeat sales. The days are gone when you could sell a product or provide a service to a customer, and you weren't concerned whether the customer was satisfied or not. Today, unsatisfied customers let the world know how they were treated, whether it is good or bad.

If your team makes every attempt to provide excellent customer service from beginning to end, you can avoid dissatisfied customers and the unnecessary actions that might result from a negative experience. Let me give an example of this.

You have a customer with whom you have a great relationship. He buys a product from you and, for some reason, the item didn't meet his expectations. He wants to return the product, but it's been opened or perhaps you have a no-return policy on that item. Do you stand firm and refuse to return the item, or do you take into consideration your previous great relationship and offer to make an exception?

If you refuse to satisfy this customer, you risk losing any future business with him. You might receive negative feedback on a website, a report to the Better Business Bureau, or even legal action. If you are smart enough to acknowledge that there is more at stake than this one item, you will provide the extraordinary customer service this situation demands. You've defused a potentially damaging problem, with the confidence that you've cemented your relationship with a valued customer, who will continue to do business with your establishment.

You need to connect the link between selling a great product and great customer service. They are equally important. You might have the best product available, but if your staff lacks effective customer service skills, you're not going to generate the sales that you desire.

The customers might not even realize they want great customer service as part of their buying experience. When they come into your business, they simply want a product that you provide. Most likely, this product is available at a variety of stores and might be offered at a better price or the same price. When they are greeted in a friendly manner, given the opportunity for assistance or explanation about the product, pay for the item with a pleasant cashier, and offered any follow up that's needed, then they are impressed and satisfied with both their purchase and their buying experience. Customers leave with a good feeling about their purchase and the people who work in your business, and they are completely satisfied with the entire transaction.

On the other hand, if you offer the best available product in the market for the best price, but the service you provide isn't great, customers might still make a purchase, but they can leave with disappointment that the business didn't really seem to appreciate them. If there was no salesperson to assist them, if the cashier was rude or inattentive, or if no one offered any help to carry the item to their vehicle, they might go home and write a bad review online, or not refer you to a friend or a colleague. Even if they purchased the product and liked it, you probably won't see that customer back in your business again.

Your staff must learn the importance of providing great customer service. One area that can really be put to the test is the guest service desk, where a person comes with a complaint or to return an item. The worst thing you can do is try to convince customers that they're wrong, that they should love the product, and they should keep it.

Customers have already made up their minds that they don't want the product; otherwise they wouldn't be there! They don't want to hear you tell them how they should feel. Perhaps they need further instructions about how to operate the product, or maybe it's defective and not performing as advertised.

You should not insult a customer's intelligence and say there's nothing wrong with the product, which causes them to feel embarrassed and perhaps become angry or defensive. In my experience, the best thing that a business owner can do is take a loss, look the customer in the eye, and say, "I will do whatever it takes to make you happy," and then wait for them to respond.

If customers feel that they have been listened to, they will know that you sincerely want their business and they won't feel cheated or mistreated in any way. They might say, "I'll be happy if you fix it." Then you fix it. If they say, "I'll be happy if you take it back," you go ahead and accept the return. If a customer comes in and says, "I'll be happy if you just get me out of it, because the product didn't do what I expected," you get them out of it.

You might be tempted to tell the customer, "Hey, if it's broken, I'll fix it." Sometimes that option will work, but at this point the customer already has a negative view of the product and you can't fix that. If you convince customers to accept a remedy that they don't really want, it's only going to create another problem later.

There's a good chance they're going to come back and say, "You told me you were able to make it work, and it doesn't." At this stage, you're going to take an even bigger loss than you would have if you had resolved the issue from the beginning and did what the customer wanted the first time. Accept the small loss in the beginning rather than risking a large loss later.

Customer service is the heart of every business. You and all of your employees need to focus on building good relationships with everyone involved in your enterprise, including clients, suppliers, and associates.

If you feel like your staff members have lost their motivation to provide good customer service, consider having a business consultant come in and give them education and training to improve their skills. Praise your employees when you see an example of them providing satisfaction to a guest. Never forget that excellent customer service is one of the fundamental building blocks of business success!

► | 15

Know Your Numbers

The budget is not just a collection of numbers, but an expression of our values and aspirations.– Jacob Lew

► | As simple as it sounds, many business owners don't know their numbers. I have known many entrepreneurs who don't know where they stand financially, and they end up in bankruptcy or are forced to close their company because they haven't managed their numbers. Some new business owners don't have any idea how much money they have until they receive their bank statement each month.

For example, in 2008 a good friend of mine started a new venture. He opened a closed-bid auto auction. What he did was simple: he was the mediator between new automotive franchises and preowned automobile dealers. A year later he expanded the business to include transactions among the new automotive franchise dealers.

This meant that a franchise dealer (such as Toyota or Honda) would be able to exchange inventory between its stores through his auction. By the second year, the company grew tremendously. It was impressive to see that his business was now doing multimillion-dollar transactions.

Later that same year, I was shocked to learn that the company had been shut down because they had issued checks totaling over $1.3 million—with insufficient funds in the bank! When I asked him what went wrong, to my surprise, his answer was, "I didn't know how much we had and how much we owed."

It was sad that a good business had been ruined by such an elementary mistake. What stood out to me the most was my friend saying, "Whatever the business needed, whatever I needed, I wrote a check for it." That goes to show you how important it is to know your numbers.

By knowing your numbers, you increase your awareness and your business increases accordingly. It's like magic!

There is something powerful about knowing exactly how much you earned, how much you owe, how much you're ahead, or how much you're behind. Knowledge is power, and you have control!

When you first open a business, you don't make money right away. It takes some time to generate income, and if you don't have a minimum reserve of six months, you're going to be struggling. Actually, six months of reserve is being quite conservative. It would be wise to have one or two years set aside, but I recognize that is not always possible.

Most new businesses don't have a large reserve of money, and if you don't have it, I personally don't think it should stop you. However, be aware that planning a budget and keeping track of your numbers is even more important if you don't have a reserve to fall back on.

You need to be aware of the numbers in all aspects of your business:

- Payroll

- Taxes

- Accounts receivable

- Accounts payable

- Inventory

- Overhead

- Other areas of your specific business

Unfortunately, employees and managers might not be honest with you. They will be tempted to tell you everything is fine when it might not be. They want you to believe everything is going smoothly so that you don't see that sales are down. There might even be an issue with an employee stealing from the company. Employees might lie, but the numbers don't lie!

When you look at the numbers, you can see where you stand. You will know if you're making a profit or if you are losing money for a specific time, be it daily, weekly, monthly, or annually. When you track the numbers on a weekly basis, or maybe a daily basis, you will know if you are meeting your goals.

This allows you to adjust and perhaps give the sales team motivation to encourage them to make an extra effort, such as phone calls to previous customers or another marketing campaign. I believe it's important to know exactly where you stand on a daily basis, because if you let a week slip by and then discover you are behind, it will be more difficult to recover.

The numbers are also important for you to be aware of to look for patterns in your sales. You will notice in which months you have the best sales, what days of the week are the busiest, and even what hours in the day you have the most customer traffic. Yes, you can actually break down your numbers into hours of the day. Knowing these numbers can allow you to provide extra employees during the rush times, to be able to facilitate those deals, and not make customers wait.

The most important numbers are how much it costs to run your business. You need to account for employee payroll, rent or lease payments, advertising and marketing costs, inventory, all taxes, utilities, internet connections and computer hardware and software, and many other expenses. There are so many costs to having a business, right?

You want to know your overhead costs, or what you have to pay out. You also want to know your income, or how much money you are bringing in. How much did we make, how much do we owe? You subtract your costs from your income, and that's your profit. If you aren't aware of these numbers, you might be in trouble. The most successful entrepreneurs are the ones who keep a keen eye on their numbers and know how to adapt to what they reveal.

► | 16

Work Hard and Smart

Wherever smart people work, doors are unlocked.

– Steve Wozniak

▶ | We've discussed how working hard is necessary for success. If you don't work hard in your business, you're not going to reach your goals, and your business will not grow and thrive! To survive in today's competitive economy, you have to give more than one hundred percent.

Mediocrity is not acceptable, because halfhearted efforts will produce halfhearted results. Be the role model that your employees will want to emulate. When they see you making smart decisions, they will realize that you are a good leader, and it will encourage them to work harder, and they will also work smarter. You might not believe your employees pay attention to how you act, but I assure you, they are always looking and assessing your behavior and how you handle business situations.

Team members observe when we are working hard. They will know if we make an unwise decision, or if we handle problems with a shrewd mind. If your employees see weaknesses in the way you operate your business, they might not respect you, and they could be prone to disregard your instructions. You have to earn the respect of your employees, and the only way you can do that is by being a hard worker and a smart worker, and an exceptional role model for them to follow.

In reality, if it were easy and you didn't have to work hard for your achievements, it wouldn't even seem like success! It feels so good to know you deserve the right to be proud of your accomplishments. There is nothing like the taste of victory when you reach your goals and fulfill your dreams, and you know you earned it.

I believe immigrant entrepreneurs have a strong work ethic. As much as I have stressed the importance of hard work, I don't think it is a huge challenge for an immigrant coming to the United States. We have a passion to make our lives better than what we experienced in our previous countries, and we're enthusiastic about achieving success. We're not afraid of hard work, and we're willing to do whatever it takes.

To succeed, we also need to focus on how to work *smart*.

What does this mean? I'll tell you.

Anyone can work hard. A man or woman can labor all day long and plow the field or haul the load. But if that person cannot increase his own productivity over time, he will never increase the value of his time. The value of your time is directly linked to your productivity.

The way humans increase their value is by working both hard and smart. We use our brains to find more efficient ways of accomplishing a task. We invent labor saving devices and we think of new processes that increase productivity. We're capable of figuring out how to plow one field today—and two fields tomorrow!

If you can discover or create methods to be faster, make things simpler, be more cost effective, find alternatives, then these are what you want to consider. These are the techniques you should consider implementing.

For example, leveraging is one of the most important tools we can utilize in our business. The word "leverage" has several different definitions, and the one I am referring to is, "influence or power used to achieve a desired result."

There are many new tools and resources geared to businesses that are available to create leverage. The primary ones that I use are online methods. You can do video marketing by creating interesting content, make attention-grabbing videos, and then put them on YouTube. There is no cost to upload your video to YouTube and you reach millions of people worldwide! That's working smart by leveraging current technologies.

You might also consider a podcast, in which you are interviewed and answer questions about your business and your products. Webinars are also an excellent method of leveraging to bring in clients or to build a list of customers. You can write a book to leverage your influence in your community and among other business leaders.

After these types of exposure, you might find that you have become a highly visible person in your field, and people will recognize who you are and the business you represent. That's working smart. That's leverage.

Another way to work smart is to make sure to hire great people. Coming from immigrant backgrounds, we might think that each of us has to be the smartest person in our business, and that's not necessarily true. As strange as it seems, you might not want to be the smartest employee in your company. Of course, you want to earn the respect of your staff, but consider that the smarter your employees are, the quicker you become successful.

If you have employees who can't make decisions on their own, drive home sales, and make suggestions that will benefit the company, then you are limiting your growth potential. You're the owner, and there's no reason to feel insecure by hiring people who are smarter than you. They can help take you to the next level of business success.

Actually, this strategy makes you really smart!

Systemizing your business is another method to work smart. Many entrepreneurs think they will have financial freedom, be able to travel, and have more time to spend with their families. This is a goal that can be reached after many years of hard work, but for the new business owner, nothing could be further from the truth.

Beginning entrepreneurs can expect to be constantly working both at the business location and at home. However, that's not necessarily good for your health and well-being. You need to be at your optimum level to guide the vision of the business and what you want to create. To do this, you can create 24/7 coverage by planning ahead to systemize the day-to-day operations. Someone, not always you, can be available to assist with the business and provide ways to improve the flow of how things are working.

When you set the foundation of your enterprise and plan for the necessary functions of your business, you will train your valuable (smart) employees to manage these systems. In this way, you can actually take time off, have a life outside of the business, and still maintain your success.

It's possible to have to best of both worlds! You have to work hard, be a good leader, utilize leverage, hire smart people, and systemize some of the processes in the business. With proper planning, it's a sure formula for success!

► | 17

Set Priorities

Good things happen when you get your priorities straight.

– Scott Caan

▶ | Setting priorities means doing the most important things first. As a business owner, setting priorities is knowing what will generate more profit and also what will generate immediate profit. I'm in the business to make money. How can I generate more money? My priorities need to be set on a daily or perhaps weekly list of things to do, depending on the business owner's decision or recommendations by management.

The other questions to follow would be: How can my priority list secure long-term growth? Does repeating the practice of making a priority list help my business and increase my wealth?

Every day, I go to work and look for ways to make my business successful and lucrative. If I made one dollar today, tomorrow I'm going to try to make two. I want my business to grow every day, every month, and every year. When a goal is achieved, another one is set. There is no limit on how high these goals can reach. Maintaining the same position that I was in last year is not an option. When I work for someone else, that might be reasonable; but I'm in business for myself, and I need to grow and constantly improve.

In order to accomplish my goal of continually progressing, I need to set priorities. To help my business continue to succeed, I want to know the most important methods and the order in which they need to be implemented. My objective is to have more income by the end of each month. I want to strive towards always increasing my profit by discovering ways to bring a higher return for my effort.

Setting priorities will increase productivity. Having a written list of the business priorities available to employees and sales personnel will increase their momentum and eventually lead to more sales.

When I present a list of priorities, my staff focuses and becomes more organized. If I went to work and didn't present any priorities, functioning as a team would become more difficult. We would all be wandering around, asking, "What are we doing today?" and answering, "We don't know. We're waiting for the phone to ring."

We need to be doing something constructive with our time and not simply waiting for someone to walk in the door or call on the phone. If you don't have a list of priorities, your employees will be forced to take the initiative to search for leads, send email messages, and make contact with potential customers. They may mean well, but they may not tackle the most important problems. When there is a set guideline for the order of what is most important, it allows your staff members to see what needs to be done, and it gives them a purpose for their time.

The best way to organize priorities is to put them in writing. One of the mistakes I made was to depend on my memory to recall everything that needed to be done. As the leader, I recognize that the way my business runs is primarily my responsibility. However, if I can't be at work for some reason, or I simply don't remember everything, the business is going to suffer if I haven't left a written a list of important tasks with a manager.

I am guilty of frequently neglecting to write down my thoughts. There have been many times that I've forgotten essential priorities because I didn't make a note. Now, I try to write things down as I think of them. Sometimes I record a voice memo to myself on my smart phone (or a handheld recorder) to keep track of my thoughts. Later I'm able to make another list, with the items organized and placed in order of importance.

To set long-range priorities, create a strategic plan. This will give your employees a view of the goals of the company over the next year or even five years. Make sure your employees know the plan, and revise it as necessary as conditions change.

Don't hesitate to delegate duties. It's easy for enthusiastic entrepreneurs to think they can do it all and believe they can manage dozens of tasks at once. If you try to do everything, it will be frustrating and you'll quickly burn out. If you are exhausted from juggling too many jobs, you might end up being unprofessional in some manner, such as speaking impolitely to a customer or employee without even realizing it.

You have taken great care to hire smart, efficient employees, and you should trust them to handle responsibilities. Of course, if there's an unexpected need, you should know all the aspects of your business and be able to fill any position. (Have you ever watched the TV show *Undercover Boss*? It's funny when the CEO attempts a front-line job like operating a cash register—but there's always a valuable lesson to be learned.). Know your business, but don't try to be a manager who has to do it all. Delegate responsibilities, and let the work be done promptly by the professionals you have trained and trust. Most people will do what you ask, and even more!

Priorities have a habit of changing, sometimes on a daily basis. What is of the utmost importance today might not be vital tomorrow. If you have regular communication with your employees and your customers, you'll be aware of what's working well and new directions you might want to consider for your business. Keep track of your ideas and implement a priority list on a regular basis. This will assist you and your staff to be the best at what you do!

▶ | 18

Do What You Know Best

Do what you love to do and give it your very best. If you can't give it your best, get out of it. Life is too short. – Al Lopez

► | Before opening your business, having experience and knowledge about that business is a crucial factor to being successful. Immigrants from different backgrounds and cultures have the disadvantage of not having time to learn how businesses in the United States operate, and the language barrier can contribute to some of this confusion.

You might be tempted to follow the same ideology or ways of doing business that you did in your previous country. Be aware that the knowledge you brought with you might be completely off-track or be an old type of thinking that just doesn't work anymore. Many of the concepts that you previously learned might come up short; they will mislead you and send you in the wrong direction, wasting time and money.

You need to refresh your ideas and mindset to embrace new ideologies and the innovative thinking that comes with your new life. Even though you have the expertise of knowing your product or your service, it is vital to learn the differences between doing that same type of business in your previous life and the new life you are starting. You should realize the importance of establishing some familiarity and proficiency in your new endeavor.

It's wonderful to have a goal to begin a business in a field in which you have experience or have enjoyed success. However, it's imperative that you don't rest on your past achievements and think that you know everything. You must be willing to alter your mindset to recognize the new rules and regulations. If you don't, it could hold you back from being successful, despite your expertise.

The best way to create this learning experience is to first get a job and be employed with an excellent company in the area that you know and love. This will help you learn how to develop a business that utilizes your existing skills. Working in an industry where you are familiar with the product or service will help you update your way of thinking. People usually succeed in the areas that they love and are excited to want to go to work. Therefore, it makes sense to be paid while you are gaining experience and increasing your knowledge.

It might seem that you are wasting time by working for someone else, but the time you spend doing this on-the-job training could save you a lot of money and headaches in your future business. If you start your own business with an old mentality that you brought with you, it could easily lead to disastrous consequences. You might lose a lot of money, or even have to shut down your operation due to not knowing a rule.

At the job, seek to find the keys to what makes a good business successful. Watch and learn the ways to conduct business in the United States. Observe the best techniques to provide excellent customer service, to give great satisfaction, and to determine what your customers expect after the sale. Discover any obstacles that you might face in this particular business, such as specific rules and regulations that require special permits, licenses, qualifications, or inspections.

How dependable are the vendors and suppliers for the products this business sells? While you're being paid, you'll find out, and you'll be able to create your own list of vendors and contacts! Use this time to learn and gather information. You'll be receiving a paycheck and also the benefits of knowledge and training to help you be a better businessperson in your own enterprise.

Don't let your ego keep you from working in a position that is less than you think your previous experience deserves.

Start at any available position within the industry that you desire. Sometimes a lesser position will give you the time to watch and learn from everything that's going on around you.

When you prove your enthusiasm for the business and show that you can bring value to the company, you can work your way up to higher positions, all the while, learning more. Take the opportunity to prove you're trustworthy and eager to learn the ins and outs of the business. Working your way through different positions in the company is the perfect way to obtain the knowledge and experience required to successfully run your own business later.

An important step toward operating your own enterprise is learning the skills required to become confident in all aspects of your field. One of the most important aspects of any type business is to learn to communicate effectively. It's not about speaking a different language, or speaking with an accent. Yes, working to reduce a heavy accent is necessary, but it's more important to learn the mannerisms and methods of successfully being understood with your body language and even your facial features.

A familiar quote says, "I can't hear what you're saying, because your actions are too loud." If you don't make eye contact, or you fumble with your phone, or you cause any actions that distracts from the conversation, then you aren't really communicating! Always give your full attention when you are interacting with other people.

As an immigrant, you deserve great credit for the hard work it takes to learn to read, write, and speak English. If you are challenged by learning a new language, an effective learning tool is listening to language tapes or finding online programs that will assist you. There are free programs available, but even if you have to pay for the services, it won't cost a lot and the rewards will be well worth it.

Don't worry if you still have an accent, as that's what makes each of us different! And when you think about it, just about everybody in America has some sort of accent. A native-born person from Georgia will speak with an accent that is very different from a native-born person from Maine or California.

Beyond knowing the language, you also need to hone your "people skills." Being comfortable and confident in your body language, in addition to your verbal skills, will enable you to communicate effectively with your coworkers, vendors, authorities, business connections, and, most important, your customers.

When you combine the idea of working in a business that you know and love, taking the time to learn how this same business works in the United States, and sharpening your communication skills, you'll soon be ready to launch your own successful company.

► | 19

Be a Problem Solver

Good management is the art of making problems so interesting and their solutions so constructive that everyone wants to get to work and deal with them. – Paul Hawken

► | Anything that causes the loss of money is a problem. It's that simple. Problems with customers, employees, vendors, accounting, and anything involved in your business will eventually lead to a decrease in revenue because of wasted time, unsatisfied customers, or the actual loss of a product.

When I first started in business, too often my idea of solving a problem was to ignore it and hope the issue would go away. I thought that time would settle things. "The customer is complaining? OK, they'll forget about it." Perhaps the customer will give up and fix it, or forget about it, and then the problem is gone.

I was inexperienced and didn't know any better. I thought running away from the problem was the answer. But now I know to never run away from a problem! In fact, it's crucial to address issues as soon as they arise. When a challenge first arises, the solution is usually easily resolved and cost-effective to fix. Once the problem escalates, customer dissatisfaction and other potential losses increase exponentially.

Immediately solving a problem makes it go away. Ignoring an issue simply allows it to fester and grow. When a problem is solved, you and your staff can return to your day-to-day business, continue productivity, keep your doors open, and maintain the focus on what's important.

In order to solve challenges in a prompt and efficient manner, you first have to identify what's wrong. What are the reasons behind the issue? Here's a true example of a problem I experienced in my car dealership, and how I worked to identify and resolve the issue.

One of my sales representatives, whom we'll call Tim, sold a great vehicle to a customer. The owner of the new car was happy with his purchase. In his attempt to sweeten the deal, Tim had promised the customer additional items that weren't discussed with or approved by the sales manager. In Tim's eagerness, he told the buyer that if he bought the car today, he could come back and get free window tint.

Tim should have consulted with the manager and explained that closing the deal might depend on adding a bonus, such as the tint. The manager likely would have told Tim to go ahead and offer the bonus to sell the car and please the customer. But even after the sale, Tim neglected to mention his additional deal to the manager.

A few days later, the customer returned to schedule the free window tint and nobody knew anything about it, except Tim. The customer, who had been very happy, was now very *unhappy*.

I had two problems, and it was crucial to address both of them immediately. The first priority was with my customer. Dealing with Tim was secondary. In this example, the problem was not with a customer or a product. I identified the problem, and it was my sales representative, Tim, who caused the confusion. The customer was not to blame. I let the customer know that whatever he was promised by Tim would be honored.

You have to show the customer that you care, and make sure they know you are willing to quickly resolve an issue. You cannot say, "Let me think about it, and we'll see what we do." You have to provide immediate relief from any discomfort the customer might be experiencing.

I took immediate action to offer the customer the option that would best satisfy him. When customer service is on the line, it's important to give various options. I offered to do the tint as soon as possible, or give him the money to get the work done at the place of his choosing. I could also have offered something else of equal value, but that wasn't necessary. By acting swiftly, I was able to salvage the relationship with the buyer, and provide the guest service that he expected.

When my customer was satisfied, then I had to deal with the root of this particular problem, which was my salesperson. Depending on an employee's work history, you can choose what you need to do. The reprimand might result in disciplinary action, a forfeiture of commission, payment for the loss that ensued, or even termination.

The employee who made the mistake needs to know that this type of miscommunication, even though perhaps not intentional, cannot be tolerated. It might even be necessary to have a meeting with your entire staff to remind them that protocol must be followed in every transaction.

In Tim's case, the cost of the glass tint was deducted from his commission, and this particular sale did not count towards his sales total in the competition to be the salesperson of the month.

Problems are tremendously time consuming. You have more important things to do than micromanage errors and mistakes. When you have staff that is trained well and management that is efficient and accurate, you've already avoided many potential problems. You won't need to focus on negative things that could be happening, and you won't waste time dealing with them.

When you see an issue, deal with it as soon as possible. The longer a situation continues, the worse it's going to get.

Another serious consideration about quickly identifying and solving problems is your health. We often refer to problems as "headaches," but they often literally *are* headaches. The stress of a lingering problem can easily cause your head to ache, in addition to other illnesses, such as high blood pressure, anxiety, ulcers, and even depression. The unresolved problem, along with the stress it brings, affects your attention and causes you to be less productive. When you can't function at your best, your business suffers.

Here's one last example of a problem you need to solve immediately: taxes. Your business needs to file federal and state income taxes, and needs to account for state sales taxes and any other taxes due. If you ever get a notice from the Internal Revenue Service (IRS) or your state department of revenue, *do not ignore it*. Open it, read it, and respond to it. If you owe taxes, the IRS and your state revenue department will probably let you set up a payment plan. Do it! Too many individuals and businesses have experienced major headaches—even bankruptcy—because they didn't fix tax problems.

You are the business owner and leader of your team. The business depends on you, and maintaining your health is vital. If your business is important to you, and I know it is, you will take care of yourself and be aware of issues that can cause stress or worry. Facing and solving problems as they arise is the best solution to resolve them. This will create satisfied customers, enlightened employees, and successful leaders for your business.

► | **20**

Build a Great Team

I'm very comfortable in having a strong team. I'm very comfortable in sharing the limelight with the team. – Sanjay Kumar

▶ | When you start your business, it is important to hire the right team. Employing the correct people to suit each job description is an essential element in building a successful business. You can't run a business without people. Entrepreneurs are energetic and optimistic, and we think we can handle everything by ourselves. Even if you plan to operate a business by yourself, such as an online venture, there will likely come a time when you need to hire assistants to help you keep things running smoothly. When you have a great team of employees, your business has the strength to grow at a faster pace.

Employees are your representatives of the company. Most of the customers coming to your establishment will not see the owner or get the chance to meet you. Primarily they will interact with the salesperson, the manager, and the cashier who completes the transaction. These are your employees and they need to represent your business with a pleasing appearance and the knowledge and experience for their specific position. These are the people who will generate the sales that your company needs to survive and grow. This team provides the service that your customers depend on. Your team represents *you*. You want the best team you can find to interpret your vision to every aspect of your business.

Having a team that will accurately interpret your voice is not only crucial from the customer's point of view, and from the sales point of view, but it is also vital to you, as the leader and owner of the business. When you have a great team, it makes your life easier. Having people you trust to take control and manage your business on a day-to-day basis allows you to concentrate on the direction your business needs to go. It gives you the time to discover new methods to expand and create new visions and goals. That's a huge benefit of hiring a good team!

For example, if you hire someone who turns out to be incompetent, you (or a manager) might have to watch him, and follow behind him to fix the mistakes he makes. Basically, you are doing his job, and you're losing money when you pay his salary for work you performed in his place, or from the time spent cleaning up the mistakes he made.

If you're taking time to watch an ineffective employee, who is covering your duties? No one can take the place of the business owner. Your name and reputation are at stake, and other people might not appreciate your position. You have to pay the bills while you strive toward a successful business, and employees do not carry the burden of responsibilities that you do.

Instead of concentrating on the tasks required of your position, you are distracted by the little issues, such as dealing with an employee who is not doing his job properly. Even if the rest of your team members are doing their jobs efficiently, the one who is not will negatively affect the whole team. You must build a team of employees who can connect with one another and work together without constant supervision.

You may have heard the saying, "Hire slow, fire fast." Don't be in a rush to fill a job opening. Find the best person. Hiring the right employees and building a great team takes a lot of time, effort, and expense. You want someone who will be a positive team member and who will stay with you for a long time.

Hiring the wrong employee can be very costly. If you don't have the correct team operating your business, it will wind up being more expensive later on. Whatever time and money you think you can save by cutting corners in the hiring process, it will end up costing you through the loss of sales, damage to your reputation, and the opportunity to flourish with a better employee.

Two different types of employees will cause damage to your business. You have to be aware of them.

The first one is simply a common thief. This person will literally get into your cash register and steal money. In today's market, that might be hard to do because payment is often made with checks, credit or debit cards, bank loans, or other non-cash methods. However, a devious person will find a way to steal from your stock, or alter the paperwork to hide inventory.

This thief might take a deposit from a customer, never give a receipt, and pocket the money. Or perhaps the crooked employee solicits a customer for money in exchange for extra services or products that would never be provided. In many cases, the business owner would never find out about it, or the employee would be gone when they do. It's unfortunate, but it happens every day in almost every type of business.

Discovering you have an employee who steals from you is crushing. At least, with a thief, you might have some recourse for recovery through the legal system.

The worst employee is the second type who damages your business, whether intentionally or unintentionally. Let's call him Ignorant. You hire him and soon realize that he is incompetent. He is not fulfilling the duties of his position, and he has a negative attitude. Ignorant wastes time and always watches the clock, waiting for his lunch break, or the time to clock out and go home.

He doesn't really care if he performed his duties or accomplished anything during the day. His lack of skills cost you sales, damages you reputation, and affects customer relations; and he is a negative influence on the rest of the team. Ignorant's actions are more damaging than the thief who steals from you and leaves!

During a few weeks, he might have caused you to lose thousands of dollars in sales and irreparable damage to your reputation. Just one employee can create dissatisfaction in a customer, which can lead to the customer giving negative reviews, effectively eliminating future sales, and harming the business that you've worked hard to build.

When you are hiring an employee, take your time. Make sure to do a background check to discover any problems with previous employers or a criminal history. You should also consider a thirty- to ninety-day probationary period. Then if you see the employee is not working out well with your business, you can dismiss him without cause.

Making the decision to fire someone is not easy. But after you have made every effort to train a substandard employee and he or she is still a problem, fire them quickly. A poor employee is a drag on your business and on the other team members who are trying their very best.

As you build your team, you need to select an exceptional person to be the manager, who can assist you with leadership responsibilities. If you have a good manager, he or she will become very valuable to you and your business. You can't physically be at work 24/7, so one or two great managers will monitor and lead your business for you.

These employees need to be trustworthy and make wise decisions in your absence and know when to call you about major issues. Your managers need to be able to handle any problems that occur in a prompt and efficient manner, to avoid loss of revenue or customer dissatisfaction. If you have a manager who thinks he is more important than the other staff, and refuses to work alongside the other employees, you need to replace him!

I think it's obvious that we need to recognize the importance of building a great team with hardworking employees. The difficult part is to find them! If you are launching a new business, you have an enormous task in finding many employees at once. If you're an existing business, it's still a challenge to fill positions that require specific knowledge, training, and experience. With either situation, you can get organized with a plan.

Once you identify an employee need, make certain you have a detailed job description for the position. It might be for a manager, a sales position, a receptionist, or any aspect of your business. Write down what you are seeking, so you will be prepared for the questions you want to ask, and the questions you will be asked.

You can post an advertisement in the newspaper or through online job sites. To avoid applicants who are not qualified, try to be as specific as possible. I've found one of the least expensive and easiest methods to find new employees is to spread the word around among friends, colleagues, and people who are in the same line of business. It doesn't cost a penny to ask for your friend's help, and they might know someone who will be a perfect fit! Obviously, you want to meet and interview any referrals. They could be the nicest person in the world, but they still might not possess the skills needed for the position.

Professional employment agencies are an option that you can consider. They have the ability to prescreen and eliminate applicants that don't meet your qualifications. There is usually a charge for utilizing agency services, but you can negotiate this fee, especially if you use the same professionals on a regular basis. Depending on the services you need, you might locate employees from online job sites or government-sponsored programs. You describe your need, they send you applicants, and you make your choices.

Occasionally other hiring options avail themselves, and here's an example of an experience I encountered. About seventeen years ago, I had a customer come into a small business that I operated, wanting to make a purchase. He was disappointed that he could not afford the item, and we began to talk about his situation. Although I could sense that he seemed disciplined and hardworking, he expressed difficulty in finding a decent job. He told me that he was loyal to every employer he'd ever had, and he always gave his heart and soul to the work.

I immediately asked him if he would like a job working for me. He was honest enough to admit that he didn't have any experience in the product that my company offered. I said, "What do you think of this idea? You give me the time, energy, and focus that my business needs, and I will show you how things work, and give you all the tools to help you succeed."

We shook hands—and seventeen years later, I still have that same employee, earning an annual six-figure salary. His position is among the most competitive in the market, and he is the best there is!

The point I'm trying to make is that you always want to hire the best people possible. Don't ignore a situation when your gut is telling you that you've discovered a person with such fantastic character that you can develop them into a professional position. Look for somebody who will arrive at work early, is eager to learn, and will be loyal and honest with you and your customers. Even though this person is not an expert in your business, if they have a good character, you can teach them what they need to know for the business. *I would always go for character versus professional expertise.* Not only have you helped a worthy person find a job, but you also have a dedicated employee who will do everything it takes to show appreciation to you!

It's time consuming and costly to hire professionals, and there might be positions in your business for which you can subcontract work. There are companies that specialize in services that they can provide to you without the liabilities and overhead of hiring an employee. An excellent example of this is janitorial services.

It's more cost effective to subcontract a janitorial service to clean your business on a regular basis than to hire an employee and stock all the cleaning supplies. It's not a key position that is needed for the survival and the growth of the business, so to subcontract this job makes great sense!

Obviously, you need employees for onsite work, such as sales, where human contact is required. Simply be aware that you have options for subcontracting work, such as managing your business's website. You don't need a person onsite to provide content for your website, handle advertising, post photos of your products, and provide a customer service link. You can find many services offered online, with negotiable prices.

You can even hire an online assistant who will be there for you 24/7. Elance.com and other websites for freelance work have a multitude of people seeking the opportunity to assist you. You post a job or service description, and freelancers from around the world bid on your job. It can be a one-time project, or a continuing service with no long-term obligation. You pay an affordable price without having the liabilities that come with hiring an employee.

As valuable as employees are, they often require expenses that go beyond their salaries. Obligations to employees often include the cost of processing their pay and taxes, worker's compensation fees, health insurance, education and training, sick days, and even scheduling vacation time. If an employee is injured on the job, there are numerous rules and regulations that you must follow, including holding open a position for them when they are able to return to work. I'm sympathetic to anyone who is hurt, but it does affect my business when I have lost a member of my team, even for a valid reason.

Hiring people with expertise and paying them an hourly wage can become costly, and most of the time businesses, especially new entrepreneurs, cannot afford to do that. My alternative to is to hire these people based on profit sharing or commission. I set a base salary that my company can afford for that particular position, and then I say, "We have the potential to reach this number. If we hit that number, then you will get two percent, three percent, or five percent." This method depends on the type of business you're in and the type of sales that you generate. Some people will be excited to work with this option, and it will be beneficial for the business, because it won't put a burden on your payroll budget.

One additional component to securing a great team is to provide ongoing education and training. Continuing education can help your staff gain knowledge of new methods and products, and it helps maintain their level of enthusiasm. Classes or seminars can involve new sales and service techniques, ways to provide additional customer satisfaction ratings, phone etiquette, people skills, and a variety of other topics.

You can find some online tips that are free, or find a speaker who will talk to your staff about being involved in what's happening in your community. You can advertise at minimal cost if you sponsor a youth athletic team or volunteer to be a part of a fundraising effort. When you are open to learning and growing, there's an endless supply of ideas.

You want a team to not only sell the product, but also sell the reputation of you and your company. We want every employee to be able to say, "We are the best at what we do. We are here to provide a good product, at a good price, and give great customer service. We're going to stand behind the product and we're going to stand behind you. That is our promise." That's what happens when you build a great team!

Part 3

Preserve Wealth

► | 21

Protect Your Assets

People protect what they love. – Jacques Yves Cousteau

► | In Part 1 and Part 2, we discussed many different ideas and suggestions for an immigrant entrepreneur to start and build a new business. These thoughts will help you make your business successful, and you can begin producing income and creating wealth. Now that you have your business started, you need to take the steps necessary to protect your assets. Your business is equivalent to your family. You love your family, you love your business, and you want to safeguard them from any harm.

To protect your assets, you have to make certain that the foundation of your business is firm and sheltered from danger. When you document any property that you own, make sure that everything is accurately described and every detail is declared on your paperwork for each specific item. Be sure to provide written proof and build a paper trail that will be easy for you and others to follow.

When you apply for a mortgage to buy a house or building for your business, a title search is part of the process. This is to assure the buyer that the title to the property is clear from any claims that previous owners might have. Almost any property can be researched back to the original owner. If you have property for which you have no clear title or ownership papers, begin immediately to rectify the situation.

Perhaps you began your business with an investor or an invisible partner. He might be working directly with you and know everything about your properties and other assets, some of which you might share the ownership. Maybe he's honest and maybe he isn't. Or maybe he isn't aware of the laws and regulations, and doing the best he can.

What happens if he decides to claim the joint assets for his own? It's your word against his. However, if your belongings have been declared, you have records on paper, and this is documentation of your proof of ownership. If you choose to accept a partner or investor, make sure that an experienced attorney reviews your contract to avoid any future disputes over assets.

Despite your precautions, you might unexpectedly be faced with a dispute. Make sure your business has proper legal protection by creating a limited liability company (LLC). An LLC is not a corporation. It's a legal method for a company that provides limited liability to its owner. This structure combines the pass-through taxation of a partnership or sole proprietor with the limited responsibility of a corporation. It helps protect your personal assets that are not business related.

Because they offer many benefits, some business owners prefer trusts. A trust is similar to a firewall between your assets and any potential problems. A new businessperson might be surprised to know the advantages of a trust. Here's an example. Instead of having my house title recorded under my name, I can create a trust, which then owns the property. I would be the trustee. This legal procedure is well known and commonly utilized among people who are already wealthy. Unfortunately, it is less known by new business people, especially immigrants.

You might think it's only your house, and it might never be affected by your business dealings, but you still want to protect it from being involved in a business dispute and therefore becoming vulnerable to a lawsuit or other claim. This is a fairly simple procedure.

It requires basic knowledge to complete a legal form and transfer the house into a trust, for the same value. It will not change the value of the house or the property taxes. Most people who have small businesses leave their houses vulnerable, because they don't know about these methods to safeguard them. If you have the funds to seek legal assistance, it will be well worth the cost.

Protecting your assets means that you are aware of laws in your state that cover you in the event of an employee or customer injury. Make sure you are up to date on worker's compensation regulations, and always carry the appropriate insurance to cover an accident that might occur on your property. These insurance policies will help prevent any lawsuits against you or your business. Make certain that your employees are aware of discrimination laws, sexual harassment regulations, and other human resources mandates that your business is required by law to observe.

Incorporate Your Business

One of the main protections I'd like to help immigrant entrepreneurs understand is the importance of incorporating your business—why you should incorporate your business, and how to go about doing it.

A corporation provides legal protection for the individuals who own and operate the business.

When we go into business, we tend to think of ourselves as a small enterprise. We're just starting out and, for a while, the company will only produce a small amount of income. If we should happen to fail in this business endeavor, it usually doesn't have a big impact. A small company just starting out will not have many assets. And it probably won't have any legal, financial, or taxation issues.

It doesn't matter if you start small; you still need to plan ahead, because you never know what might happen. You don't want to presume that your business won't need to be protected for a year or two, and you can wait to incorporate later. A situation might occur that you need protection!

Sometimes it might take months to process applications, obtain licensing, get inspections, and adjust your business plan. Look beyond where you're beginning and see where you want to be. By the time you get your incorporation processed, you might have already grown your business at a phenomenal rate, and you will be thankful that you have been protected from the start. Have the vision to consider unforeseen obstacles and be ready to handle them should they occur.

Even if you don't think you need to incorporate your business right away, when you do need it, you'll have to hustle to get all the paperwork completed and filed. As with many permits and licenses, regulations and zoning can be changed. At a certain moment, you might have an opportunity to make extra profits, but you won't be able to take advantage of it because you don't have the proper licensing. Perhaps then you didn't think you had extra money to spend to incorporate, but now you're losing thousands of dollars.

Time goes quickly and, before you know it, several years have passed. Your business has grown along with the liabilities. If you've waited to incorporate, it might be too late to have the legal protection it gives you, and that would be a painful lesson to learn.

You don't want to build your business based on the idea of limiting yourself to a small-business mentality. All the immigrant entrepreneurs I know dream big! You can envision a huge corporation, with everybody buying into it, and it's worth millions of dollars. When you dream it, you know that it is possible!

When you envision the future, it's worth it to spend a few hundred dollars to incorporate your business to protect your assets. This is money well spent. Incorporation is similar to an insurance policy, and you wouldn't think of driving your car without insurance, or being without health or homeowner's insurance.

We need the peace of mind and the reassurance to be in place for growth, for protection, and for expansion. You might begin as a small store, but it's possible to reach your dream of earning big profits and creating wealth that you can hardly imagine. The motivation is the idea of having a corporation, and you are the president or the chief executive officer (CEO).

This provides the momentum to keep going, and gives you a feeling of excitement that you are going to be successful. Incorporation allows you to choose a business name that is protected from being used by anyone else. You will be able to declare the use of that name, to receive legal business acknowledgment to obtain licensing and open a bank account with your business name.

The more legitimate the structure of your business is, the better chance that your business will grow and be ready to expand.

Once you have one corporation established, it only covers certain things. You will need different licensing from different authorities for different items.

You might think, "I just need a license to sell my ABC product." If you look ahead, you will consider that you might also eventually want to sell the DEF product. A few more years later you'll be ready for GHI products, and eventually all the way to XYZ.

If you think small and only do the minimum licensing that's required by the city, the county, the state, or other governmental authorities, you have limited your potential growth. Once opportunity arises, it's often open for a brief time, and you might not get another chance. Don't wait to get the proper licensing and file the necessary legal documentation.

In the United States, there are three basic types of corporations. They are created by state laws.

C corporation. A corporation is a separate legal entity set up under state law that protects owner assets from creditor claims. Incorporating your business automatically makes you a regular, or "C" corporation. A C corporation (or C corp) is considered to be an individual taxpayer, with income and expenses taxed to the corporation and not to the owners. If corporate profits are then distributed to owners as dividends, each owner must pay personal income tax on the distribution, creating "double taxation" (profits are taxed first at the corporate level and again at the personal level as dividends). Many small businesses do not opt for C corporations because of this tax feature.

S corporation. Once you've incorporated, you can elect S corporation status by filing a form with the federal Internal Revenue Service (IRS) and with your state, if applicable, so that profits, losses and other tax items pass *through* the corporation to you and are reported on your personal tax return. The S corporation itself does not pay tax.

Limited liability company (LLC). Another business type that is formed under state law and gives you personal liability protection is the LLC. Tax-wise, an LLC is similar to an S corporation (or S corp), with business income and expenses reported on your personal tax return. If you are the only owner of an LLC, you are viewed as a "disregarded" entity. This means you report the LLC's income and expenses on Schedule C of Form 1040—the same schedule used by sole proprietors.

In order to become incorporated, paperwork needs to be filed with your state government, and a fee paid. The average person doesn't know how to do this properly and should not attempt it without legal assistance. You should either:

1. Consult a lawyer or accountant who specializes in business law, or

2. Use a reputable service such as LegalZoom. For example, LegalZoom will take you through a three-step process:

a. Complete the incorporation questionnaire.

b. Then, LegalZoom creates and files your incorporation papers with the Secretary of State in your state.

c. When LegalZoom receives your filed Articles of Incorporation back from the state, they send them to you along with the rest of your formation documents, as well as easy instructions regarding next steps.

Some states have no charge for a business to be incorporated. Check with the state that you're doing business in to discover if there are fees. If you research the fee that the state charges, then you know any money above that amount is going to the person who is providing the paperwork.

That's why I suggest you can negotiate the charges. You can explain that you're starting your business and the budget is tight. Offer to give him your future business. If you're working on the incorporation process with an accountant, you'll need someone to do your bookkeeping and file taxes, and other financial needs, so most accountants are smart enough to realize the benefit of negotiation!

The same applies to an attorney. You will want to establish a relationship that can be ongoing so you can have the benefit of legal representation for issues that might arise in the future. It's better to have someone who you can call on, if you need them, before a problem arises.

As one immigrant entrepreneur to another, I've been asked, "What are the benefits to incorporating my business?" The bottom line is that incorporation is the only way to go to protect your investment. There is no way around this. To take the risk of putting your own name on your business is gambling with your personal credit rating, your house and personal property, your spouse's assets, and your children's future. Don't take this risk!

Have you seen any successful, multimillion-dollar business that does not work under legal incorporation? It does not exist. Any entrepreneur who asks for my advice will hear this: "The first money you should spend, even if you're an in-home business or a small business, must be to establish your corporation." Otherwise, in the event of a legal dispute, people can collect from you personally and seize your assets. The person you're dealing with in the dispute might not even care about your business. If they can freeze your bank accounts and tarnish your good name, they are going to try to ruin you!

If you are an incorporated business, others cannot touch your personal assets; they can only go after the business assets. I hope my passion regarding the importance of this aspect has reached your business mind. Many new business owners don't even know about incorporations, or they try to save money by procrastinating and say that they'll do it later.

In California, the cost to incorporate is $800. That might seem like a lot of money, but you're buying insurance so that you will be protected. You're avoiding potential headaches for this sum. It distresses me that a successful businessperson might have to say, after being involved in a dispute, "If I knew then what I know now, I would happily spend $8,000, if I had the chance to go back and put my business under a corporation." Be smart and protect your assets by every means available to you!

► | **22**

How to Avoid Headaches

A great wind is blowing, and that gives you either imagination or a headache.– Catherine the Great

▶ | It's often tempting to run away from problems, and avoid the headaches that are bound to occur in any business. How do you deal with problems? In Part 2, "Be a Problem Solver," I addressed the importance of confronting problems and dealing with them immediately. Any time you avoid dealing with any issue or try to postpone it, sooner or later it will escalate into a more difficult situation and it's eventually going to catch up.

From my experience, I've learned if I get a phone message that there is a problem, whether it's an unhappy customer, an audit, or a sick employee, I call back as soon as possible to get the necessary information to process and defuse the situation as soon as possible.

When I know the specifics of the problem, that information automatically releases half my stress. If I know the facts, it's a great relief to be able to move forward on getting the matter resolved.

You need to be wise in determining when it's necessary to seek professional help through an attorney or an accountant. There are situations when you should keep your distance from the resolution of a problem, and let a person more knowledgeable handle it for you. If you attempt to try to solve something that you never solved before, you might wind up making things worse.

The money you thought you saved by not hiring a professional could cost you your entire business. There are also considerations of lost time, possible confrontations with angry people, and the stress and frustration about dealing with unusually difficult situations.

I have been fortunate in becoming a prosperous businessman. As I've mention throughout this book, I've made mistakes and learned many things on the road to success. I'm often asked about the traits that got me where I am today. The main reason I wanted to write this book is because many other entrepreneurs often call me for advice, and I believe my experiences and my thoughts will benefit others.

Probably the most important idea I try to emphasize is that you should use your common sense. If something seems good, it probably is. If it seems too good to be true, it probably is. Follow your gut feeling when you're making choices, because it's probably right!

A good example of this common sense advice is to stay away from "easy money." For instance, if you normally pay one dollar for a product and someone is offering the same exact product for twenty-five cents, this should send up a "red flag" that you need to stay away! Your gut feeling is telling you that there is something fishy about this deal. Even if it appears to be one hundred percent legitimate, papers can be forged and other documentation about the product can be faked.

Let me share with you something that I experienced at my car dealership.

A man came to my dealership and offered to sell me a car for $15,000. I knew the car was valued at $30,000 and I thought, "This man is either desperate for money or he's unintelligent." It was one of those deals that I knew was too good to be true, but he insisted on following through, so I knew I needed to take extreme precautions.

. The man had a valid document from the Department of Motor Vehicles (DMV), proving a completed transaction with them.

A few weeks later, I sold the car, and was happy at the profit margin of this specific transaction.

Then the "authentic proof of ownership" was discovered to have been fraudulently established. The papers that the man took to the DMV were forged, but he had enough information to get an actual title, and the DMV mistakenly thought it was original. There was a paper trail, but it was discovered too late to avoid the loss that incurred.

The next thing I knew, an official was knocking at my door and saying, "Pay up." I had sold a car that didn't belong to me, and, regardless of the precautions I had taken, I had to take the loss. I had the option to attempt to find the person who sold it to me and make him pay me back, but that's next to impossible. This example could be devastating for a small business that hasn't prepared for rainy days.

The moral of this story is to stay away from something that doesn't make sense. If the circumstances seem unrealistic, or too good to be true, it's a red flag. Occasionally we will encounter a fantastic deal, but the vast majority of the time we have to work hard to be profitable. There are no short cuts on the road to success.

We have to work hard *and* smart. Now, if someone approaches me with a deal and I'm not comfortable with it because my gut feeling is that something is wrong, I stay away from it. I don't take unnecessary chances.

People ask me how to avoid legal issues. I tell them that they are part of doing business and unavoidable. There's always going to be issues. When you deal with the general public, no matter how organized a corporation is, there will be issues that must be handled through legal procedures.

Things happen, laws change, and something you didn't even know existed will arise and affect your business. You have to be alert and use common sense when seeking legal representation. As with my advice on dealing with any problem or headache, confront legal issues as soon as possible.

When you realize you need to hire an attorney, seek one who has experience in the specific matter that is involved. I also advise that you get the best lawyer available that you can afford. The best lawyer will have years of experience, a great success rate, astonishing clientele, and vast recommendations. The extra amount of money you spend for a stellar attorney will pay off in your peace of mind, knowing your issue is in great hands.

It's likely that you can find an attorney who will charge you less than the best, and it's tempting to cut corners and try to save money. What was the less expensive choice might end up costing more, through incompetent representation, additional time, and hidden fees that weren't in the original cost.

You've turned everything over to the attorney, and you can go back to your business and not worry about the issue. There is always the chance that even an excellent attorney will not succeed in your favor. If you hired the less expensive one, you would always wonder if he did a good job. With the best representation possible, you don't have to wonder about that issue. You will be able to know you hired the best person for your situation.

Of course, I'm not telling you something that you've never heard before. I'm sharing a lifetime of experiences and facts about things that happened to me. I can relay hundreds of stories, with hundreds of lessons to be learned. You need to remember that everyone can learn and benefit from their mistakes. My aim is to let some of those mistakes be from lessons I've experienced, and save you the pain, loss, and defeat of experiencing them for yourself.

Invisible Partners

One of my biggest struggles in becoming an entrepreneur in the United States was learning about what I refer to as "invisible partners." I had to grasp the fact that the money I earned needed to be divided into pieces to distribute in various directions to these invisible entities. Invisible partners are entities you might not have to deal with on a daily basis, but they exist within your business. They range from multiple government agencies, to dealing with complaints, lawsuits, injuries, even to problems with employees.

Initially I viewed these agencies as enemies who were always there to regulate my business. In some instances, you can deal with the invisible partners by adjusting your mindset. When you learn how to split your profit and satisfy their demands, you will be in a much better position to focus on your business. You will be more productive and at the same time obtain peace of mind, which will eliminate those sleepless nights.

You can make invisible partners your enemy or you can make them your friend. It might be a matter of recognizing selfishness inside yourself, because you'd rather not give your hard-earned money to these partners. The best way I found to deal with invisible partners is to recognize that they get a cut of your profits. You have to accept the fact that they are there for the interest of both the consumer and the business owner, and they will come and collect what you owe them.

Probably my biggest failure in business was ignoring the invisible partners, and pretending that I could outsmart them and play my own way. It only takes a few times of not paying them what is due and you can cripple or often lose your business because you've chosen to ignore their demands.

It will affect you emotionally, mentally, and even physically. Keep in mind that if you fail, they fail too, because they're your partners. They don't want you to fail. I learned this the hard way, and now I recognize they are not my enemy. It is in their best interest for you to keep your business doors open, because they cannot exist without your tax contributions.

I'm certain that I have not come close to addressing the multitude of the headaches that you will encounter as you begin your new endeavor. Each business will have its own individual problems and solutions. I hope that the few examples I've shared and the acknowledgment of the mistakes I made will assist you in becoming a more successful entrepreneur.

► | 23

Seek Qualified and Skilled Advisors

Choose wise people for your advisors, and allow only them the liberty of speaking the truth. – Niccolò Machiavelli

▶ | Many immigrant entrepreneurs starting a business think that they cannot afford professional advisors. If you are purchasing an existing business, you require someone knowledgeable to review the accounts and a lawyer to make sure the transaction is a sound investment. If you are buying or renting a building, you must have an experienced real estate professional to ensure the papers are drawn up correctly.

When you have a knowledgeable accountant and an experienced lawyer, this will provide a solid foundation, and then you can move forward with the process of operating a day-to-day business. You have the comfort and assurance that your investment is protected by the professionals who will guide you in your financial matters and assist you with following the proper procedures.

For the majority of immigrants who arrive in the United States with limited resources, it's unlikely that they'll be able to afford the best accountants and the best attorneys at first. There are different methods you can utilize to do the best with what you have.

Compared to twenty-five years ago when I began, most of the information we need is simply a click of a button away. If you are not computer savvy, ask for assistance from a friend or relative who knows their way around the internet. Take the time to learn how to perform a search for the questions you need answered.

With modern technologies, information is readily accessible. There is information on government regulations, laws, tax information, and almost anything you need to know. Most of this information, if not all, is provided on state and federal government sites. If you can't afford to hire someone, you can still manage to function. You simply have to do it yourself until you can afford to engage a professional.

Keep in mind that government agencies, whether for permits, licenses, or taxes, want you to stay in business to boost the local economy! They are happy to provide information about how to protect yourself, because they don't want to put you out of business on some technicality because your taxes and license fees pay them and allow them to function.

If I have an issue with any taxation, from either state or federal, I can go to the appropriate website and get all the forms and information that I need. I can call the hotline regarding my specific issue. I can seek advice about how to get the correct forms and they will instruct me on what to do. There are many sites and blogs about people who have been through the same issues you might be facing. With a bit of online research, you can find the majority of what you need to know.

Even if you have the resources to hire an attorney and an accountant, it's always in your best interest to take the time to learn and educate yourself, or someone in your facility, about matters that concern you the most. You can search online and find the information you need. For example, you might have concerns that your accountant hasn't allowed credit for some exemptions, or perhaps you're wondering if the deductions are common for your type of business.

Maybe the only accountant you can afford mainly deals with restaurants, but you're in the clothing industry. He's not going to turn you away, but he doesn't have experience or knowledge about your business, and he might miss some exemptions or deductions that are specific to your industry. To make matters worse, if you are audited, he would bail out.

In the meantime, it is your responsibility to bear. You're the one in trouble and you are required to pay penalties, back taxes, interest, and lost time for dealing with the dilemma.

Unfortunately, I have personal experience in a situation like this. I trusted my accountant and never bothered to check behind his reports. After ten years, he told me, "I cannot handle your accounts. It's beyond me, and you need to look for an accountant who specializes in your type of work." That was the first I knew of him struggling to do my accounting, and it was a shock to learn that he had done many things wrong, especially during a tax audit.

I would have saved myself a lot of headaches if I had done some research before I hired him. Luckily, the government agency took into consideration the fact that he was incompetent, because it was obvious from the way he had done things improperly.

Not all certified public accountants (CPAs) are qualified to deal with tax audits, nor have the knowledge and experience to handle one. If one of my kids is sick, I would want to have the best medical team examine and treat him with the best medicine available. Wouldn't you do the same? It is no different here. My business is a member of my family.

You should always try to find out as much as you can about professionals before you hire them. Find a person with good reviews on business sites, and someone who specializes in your specific type of business. In my case, I was able to find a professional who knew my business, and had experience with my needs; and I was pleasantly surprised to find his rates were less expensive than the inept accountant.

If you don't have the budget to allow you to hire the best person possible, at least find out as much as you can about people, even vendors and other companies you deal with. The time you use doing research will be time well spent!

► | **24**

Set Aside Money for Rainy Days

The shortest period of time lies between the minute you put some money away for a rainy day and the unexpected arrival of rain.

– Jane Bryant Quinn

►| In a previous section, I mentioned the concept of invisible partners and the many hands that are reaching for part of your money. This is the idea I like to utilize when setting aside money for a rainy day, or an unexpected expense. Create several bank accounts; allocate each account to one of these invisible partners. You can even make up a name for these invisible partners, if it helps you relate to the concept!

The idea is that you add money in these accounts, but you can't use the money because it belongs to the invisible partner. Obviously, it's under your name because you created the accounts, and you make the deposits.

If you need to use some of the money, remember that it is not yours. You are using your partner's money. Maybe you found a good investment and you've "borrowed" the money from your invisible partner's account. When your investment pays off, you need to put the money back into your partner's account, and make sure to include the profit you made from the investment. He's going to know you used his money, and he's not going to forgive you for using his money if you don't return it, with interest.

Issues will come up, and you might need money, and your invisible partner's fund is that currency, which you've essentially set aside for a rainy day. You might have an important need in your business, or a lawsuit, or an emergency of any nature. In a way, you are acting as your own insurance company for a rainy day. From time to time you might need to borrow money from the invisible partner, but it's imperative that you return the funds as soon as you can, to secure the safety net.

If I am able to allocate twenty or twenty-five percent of my income to the invisible partner's account, I'm not going to be stressed when it has to be collected. That money was never mine. It's part of doing business, and now I have the freedom to continue to focus on my business. I like to use the idea of the invisible partner's involvement to remove the idea of extra money from my mind.

If you're a smart, strong businessperson, who is disciplined in being frugal and setting aside money for rainy days, you don't need to entertain this method, which works for me. Instead of allotting money to different accounts, you reach the same results within your bookkeeping system. It might be all in one bank account, but you know that a certain percentage of that money is not yours to spend.

Either way, when you need funds for an emergency, it's available. During a periodic inspection, you might need to repair a door for a required safety exit. Perhaps you weren't up to the latest code on handicap parking signs or spaces and you need to correct that situation. The fire department might come and notice a situation that is deemed unsafe or a potential fire hazard. In order to meet their requirements, you must hire a professional, such as licensed electrician, to fix the problem. All of a sudden, you're out thousands of dollars, and your budget is ruined.

I realize it's hard for a small business owner, who is just beginning, to allocate money to a fund that is not dedicated for immediate use. Remember that the money you should set aside for a rainy day is in proportion to the size of your business. If you have a seven-figure gross income business, that account has to match accordingly. For a small business, that fund can start small. For example, if you have $1,000 in revenues from your business, you should allocate $250 or more, which is twenty-five percent or higher of what your business is worth. That percentage is not going to make a difference in your profit. If you can set aside more than twenty-five percent, that would be better.

My advice would be that if you start your business with $40,000, set aside $10,000 of that money in your invisible partner's account for those rainy-day emergencies. Twenty-five percent might not be possible, but it's a goal to strive to reach.

We all want to make money, and it could be tempting to use all the funds available to bolster the inventory. You might even think that you can avoid paying a bill or your quarterly taxes in order to have extra funds to buy goods or pay bills. This is not a good idea.

Another approach to examine the situation is not to have all your investment tied up in your inventory. What if the product doesn't sell? You're going to be stressed, which compounds your ability to run your business. You find yourself going backward instead of forward, and you don't have a safety net to catch you. When there is nothing to save you, you could lose your business.

Business Insurance

Another thing to mention that is of great importance is business insurance. All of us have insurance on our cars, our houses, and even our belongings. Some of us also have life insurance. We recognize the importance of having it.

In the business world, I consider it mandatory to have insurance, and it must include full coverage to cover all aspects of the business. In my current business, I have every kind of coverage offered by the insurance companies.

For example, I have coverage against fraudulent checks, false identification (identity theft), misrepresentation of documents, employee theft, discrimination, and the traditional coverages of theft, fire, and other damages. Most business owners don't even know that some of these coverages exist.

And some owners might think that they don't need all this insurance. However, in the past seven years, my businesses has endured losses equaling 240 percent of the total cost of the insurance policies. Don't we need to secure our businesses, our life savings, and our sources of income? Indeed, we do.

As entrepreneurs, it's in our nature to want to grow quickly, and we desire a position where we are making a lot of money in a brief amount of time. We want to get to the place of importance where we see other successful businesses, and we want to have the money they have. The lure of becoming rich is intoxicating, and it's understandable that you are envious of the prosperous businesses around you.

While it will be tempting to take risks to bring in more profits, the potential for loss is so great that you must be wise and avoid disastrous results. You will not only suffer financial loss, but the stress and headaches you create will affect you, your family, and even your employees, who depend on you for their living. And don't forget the creditors, as they will continue to demand payment from you.

Setting aside money to assist your business in the event of an emergency is a vital component to a successful business. In my opinion, this is a fundamental building block to the foundation of your endeavor. Look at the big picture and set money aside for when you might really need it.

► | 25

Reinvest Profits and Diversify

It's far better to buy a wonderful company at a fair price than a fair company at a wonderful price. – Warren Buffett

▶ | When you're years into your investment or your venture, hopefully there comes a time when you are very successful. You don't need more inventory or stock to produce sales. You're saturated for the size of the company that you have. This means that you can start generating more income that leads to savings.

We know that idle money doesn't produce a profit. If keep your eyes open for opportunities to reinvest or to generate more money, they will always come along.

I'd like to share this story. A friend of mine is a multimillion-dollar producer in a real estate club. She's a great investor and real estate agent who's been in the business for more than twenty years and has participated in many real estate deals. She has all the knowledge and all the experience that is required to know a good opportunity when she sees one.

I met her in 2001, when she helped me with the purchase of my dream house. We remained friends, and by 2007 I had some money put away and was looking for a way to diversify. We went into a joint venture together on a piece of commercial property. Even though she had the expertise for this type of business investment, and I had all the trust in her, I still had to do the research and make sure the risk was not too high for me. I studied all my steps before I felt comfortable to accept the offer.

Later, we had some guidance to subdivide the property, and we sold it and made a significant return on investment. That was a great thing for me to experience, as it opened a new door. This was a new way for me to diversify and to learn that there are higher profit margins in other markets or industries.

Why It's Important to Diversify and Reinvest Profits

The first reason to diversify is to increase the profit. It is essential to test other markets to see the return on investment (ROI) in that business. I know the ROI for my business and I can compare it to the new venture. This helps increase the profit by having diversified funds in several different types of businesses. Of course, it's not rocket science—the more you invest, the more money you should have back in return, if the investment is going in the right direction.

The second reason is that diversify means that all your business is not just with one type of industry. You might remember the big Blockbuster video stores. We used to take a drive in the evening to just rent a movie or a video game for our kids. These stores were everywhere and it was fun to meet there to pick out our movies. Then we'd go home and watch them. Now, we sit at home in the comfort of our living room and pick out a movie through Amazon, Netflix, Hulu, and others.

What happened to Blockbuster? They were driven out of business. We don't want to be in that situation where we only have one kind of industry to depend on and we only have one type of income. If we diversify, it protects us from situations such as the Blockbuster collapse. If we have several investments, and one of them doesn't perform well, such as the ROI was very low or perhaps endured losses, we shift and direct our focus to another business that we currently have. We're not out of business—we are still in business and producing income. Then we go diversify again and find another industry or another market to direct our attention to.

A third reason why diversifying is important is that it opens new possibilities to us through other professions or industries—not only those that might have a greater impact of

ROI, but also a venture that our inner souls might be better at. So, for example, I could be in the type of business that neither my education nor my professional background has been involved in.

For example, I would love to be involved in online business or maybe even write a book. But for the past twenty-five years I've been in the business of selling automobiles, automotive parts, and repairs. However, a new possibility supports your soul and increases your happiness in life, which is important to be able to learn and grow emotionally.

It is important to follow your dreams, especially when you're achieved one goal with a successful business and your financial situation is comfortable. This allows you more opportunities to perhaps take more of a risk or look for higher ROI. You can do this because it's self-fulfilling, or perhaps it's an emotional satisfaction, or it's something that you always dreamed of doing. You couldn't do it previously because you couldn't afford the risk, so it didn't make much sense.

We're all involved in business to generate money and wealth. So after being financially set, the doors of possibilities open. You can find something that might generate income or it might give you the emotional satisfaction of fulfilling your dream. If you can afford it and it gives you pleasure, why not follow your dreams and your heart? Do the things you love versus the things that you don't.

All successful immigrant entrepreneurs need to diversify. I encourage you to look for good opportunities. Study the risks and the ROI and see where it goes!

► | 26

Don't Get Caught Between Two Worlds

Between two evils, I always pick the one I never tried before.

– Mae West

▶ |Immigrant entrepreneurs face many challenges. As excited as you are to arrive in the United States with your enthusiasm and visions for your future, there will be many distractions, such as learning new customs and the language. Getting settled in your new country and working in a new business is about concentration and focus.

Center your attention on building one business, in one place, until you are established. Once you get the foundation set, if your business is successful, it will grow, whether from expanding your existing location, adding multiple stores, or building a variety of businesses with different divisions.

Being caught between two worlds can be interpreted as figurative or literal. There is no need for immigrants to give up their previous languages, customs, and traditions. There's nothing wrong with honoring your heritage and keeping your native country close to your heart. Immigrants who resist learning the language or the customs that are celebrated embody the more figurative meaning of being caught between two worlds.

The literal definition of being caught between two worlds would encompass the immigrants who still maintain a business in their previous country. It's understandable that you would want to keep the income from that business and to maintain a positioning status within that community. However, when this happens, you can literally find yourself caught between the two worlds.

It's hard enough to try to build a successful business in one country. Attempting to juggle two businesses in two different countries will cause you to lose the concentration and focus that is required to gain or maintain lasting success. Losing precious time, going back and forth, will affect your production and your sales, because you can't give each place the full attention it deserves.

Time away from the business, travel expenses, jet lag, and many other factors can become extremely costly, and you are likely negatively affecting both businesses and the chance for growth and success. You need to make a decision on which business is more important and where you want to focus your energy. By making a choice, you will discover you have more time to be more productive, successful, and prosperous.

I believe the decision is easy. It's a matter of setting priorities, and perhaps the priority is the United States, where you know there is more opportunity and more room for growth. Give your full attention to your new business until it is fully developed, growing, and prospering.

Perhaps you can turn the business in your native country over to a trusted family member or colleague, until you find a time when you can have the energy and resources to determine if you can make both businesses work.

Trying to keep a business running successfully in two different countries will take away the assets and the savings that could be invested in one stronger business. Each new business needs the utmost care and all your available resources, and even then, there will still be struggles and challenges. You can only truly devote yourself to one business and one country, and not expend your time, energy, and money traveling back and forth.

Even if you have money to secure the new business, it needs your leadership and your vision to help it succeed. You might have the best managers and staff members, and they are loyal and trying their best to help your business become successful. They are not *you*. Their names are not on the business, the loans, or the assets. If you leave for even brief periods, by the time you come back, you'll find that the business is suffering from your lack of leadership, direction, and vision.

Your staff might have feelings that your other business is more important to you than the new one, and feel betrayed. A dishonest employee could take advantage of your absence and embezzle funds or steal from you in other ways. Feelings of abandonment, apathy, and other negative attitudes can infect and grow among your staff. There are many reasons that your staff morale would suffer while you are gone, devoting your attention elsewhere.

Perhaps the reason you want to keep a business in your native country is to maintain your status in the community. If so, there are other methods to achieve the standing you seek. Select a worthy foundation or a charity in your community where you can allocate funds to support that cause.

Your name will be recognized as a contributor and a valued person for your philanthropy. Show your support for community needs through fundraising events and other activities that will recognize your funding and secure your devotion to the community, thus ensuring the community status you want to keep.

A part of us calls us to our roots and the connections we have. It is important to keep that relationship, along with your customs and your traditions. But when it comes to a business decision, you should never to look back. Follow your dreams by putting all your efforts in your new country's business.

Stay with your current business and don't let that nostalgic feeling sway you, particularly from a business vantage. Regardless of where you reside, it is important to set standards for your life. Honor your previous country, but make diligent efforts to become familiar and respect your new culture. Working hard, with all your heart and soul, will allow you to establish a new business and achieve unlimited success.

► | Conclusion

To succeed, you will soon learn, as I did, the importance of a solid foundation in the basics of education—literacy, both verbal and numerical, and communication skills. – Alan Greenspan

Twenty-six years ago I immigrated to the United States, seeking wealth, success, a better life for me, and a secure future for my children. I also wanted a better education for me and for them. Here's the basic concept—it was doable, and I did it. Everybody can do it. I chose to take this road, just like you did. If I did it and succeeded, then you can do it.

I'm an immigrant entrepreneur. English is my second language. We basically come from the same background, the same education, the same mentality, the same expectations, the same experiences, more or less, and we have the passion and drive to have great success in our lives!

Immigrants to the United States have a higher percentage of business ownership than non-immigrants among the working force. This is the land of opportunity, and when we come here, each of us looks for key opportunities to create and build a business for our success.

Conclusion

It's not an easy journey, as there will be hardships and obstacles, and the rate of business failures is high. But if you will follow the strategies in this book and protect yourself and your investment, you can succeed and have great wealth.

If you have the will, the opportunities are everywhere. Be aware that while your first business venture might not lead to wealth, it will give you the business experience and knowledge that you need to begin another business venture. Your greatest success might not come until your third or fourth business venture. It's learning through experience and gaining wisdom.

The greatest thing about being an immigrant and starting a new venture is that there is no limit for your success. There are no limitations for the size of your business or the wealth and greatness that can be accomplished. Many immigrant entrepreneurs have accomplished great success with an incredible amount of money. But, most of us don't start out with an abundance of money, so it is your hard word and your willingness to work with the strategies in this book that will help you grow your business. Don't forget to take a break, enjoy the journey, and make sure you're learning form the experiences.

At the end of the day, it's not how much money you put in your bank account. It's more about who you become on your journey of discovery, of self-awareness, and of self-development; it's an evolution to a higher consciousness. Once you learn how to make money and create wealth, even if you lose it all, you can always make more.

Entrepreneurship is a challenging road, and it doesn't always go the way you planned. I hope you take what you've learned in this book to help you avoid the struggles and challenges that I went through. With the suggestions that you've learned and the knowledge you have acquired to create a solid foundation for your business ventures, I know you're on your way to great success!

I wish you the best on the new journey, including health, wealth, love, joy, and prosperity.

► | Appendix

Immigrant Groups Who Become Small-Business Owners

Did you ever wonder which immigrant groups start the greatest number of businesses?

As a percentage of new arrivals, Greek immigrants are more likely to become small-business owners than immigrants from any other country.

According to a report from the Fiscal Policy Institute's Immigration Research Initiative, using data from the U.S. Census Bureau, there are 75,000 Greek immigrants in the U.S. labor force. And of those, 16.1 percent are small-business owners. This tops immigrants from Israel at 13.2 percent, Syria at 12.1 percent, Iran at 11.8 percent, and Lebanon at 11.3 percent.

NATIONALITY	PERCENT OF IMMIGRANTS WHO START BUSINESSES
Greece	16.1
Israel/Palestine	13.2
Syria	12.1
Iran	11.8
Lebanon	11.3
Jordan	10.8
Italy	9.9
Korea	9.8
South Africa	9.2
Ireland	8.2
Iraq	8.2
Pakistan	8.2
Turkey	7.7
Argentina	7.3
Egypt/UAR	6.8
Taiwan	6.8
England	6.6
Cuba	6.5
Venezuela	6.3
Canada	6.2

If you're wondering about Mexico, while 105,000 immigrants to the U.S. from that country are small-business owners, they account for only one percent of Mexican immigrants' total labor force in the U.S. Perhaps this is because so many Mexican immigrants come to join family members, or simply to work and send money home.

Immigrant-owned businesses contribute greatly to the U.S. economy. Immigrants have high business formation rates, and many of the businesses they create are very successful, hire employees, and export goods and services to other countries. Insuring sufficient access to financial capital is important for the continued contribution of immigrant-owned businesses to economic growth, job creation, innovation and exports.

Although recent research documents the contributions of immigrant entrepreneurs to the U.S. economy, less attention has been drawn to the advantages and disadvantages that immigrant entrepreneurs face in creating and maintaining successful businesses. A better understanding of the constraints faced by immigrant entrepreneurs may shed light on whether there is untapped potential for this group and whether their contributions to the U.S. economy can be even greater. Furthermore, identifying potential barriers to financial capital access for any group of small business owners is extremely important for avoiding losses in economic productivity.

One area in which knowledge is especially lacking is access to and use of financial capital among immigrant entrepreneurs. Anecdotal evidence suggests that instead of banks or other institutions, immigrant entrepreneurs rely heavily on informal sources to finance their businesses, but there is little direct evidence from nationally representative datasets carefully documenting these patterns. An exception is provided by Census data suggesting that there may be significant leveraging of personal wealth by immigrant entrepreneurs.

—Matt Vasilogambros and Stephanie Stamm
National Journal, August 27, 2014

▶ | About the Author

Ahmad Farhat is an entrepreneur who emigrated from Lebanon to the United States in 1988. In 1996 he received a bachelor of science degree in electrical, biomedical and clinical engineering from California State University, Long Beach. Even though Farhat has an engineering background, he spent many years working in sales. In this role, he used his scientific mindset and reasoning skills to adapt a new strategy to solve problems and fulfill the needs of others.

A successful businessman with a variety of interests, Farhat is proud owner of a profitable automotive dealership, is a real estate investor, and operates several online companies.

A man of faith, Farhat is blessed with a wonderful, supportive wife and four beautiful children.

www.ingramcontent.com/pod-product-compliance
Lightning Source LLC
Chambersburg PA
CBHW051804170526
45167CB00005B/1880